WEß PAGE DESIGN
in easy steps

Brian Austin

COMPUTER
STEP

In easy steps is an imprint of Computer Step
Southfield Road . Southam
Warwickshire CV33 OFB . England

Tel: 01926 817999 Fax: 01926 817005
http://www.computerstep.com

Reprinted 1999
First published 1998

Notice of Liability
Every effort has been made to ensure that this book contains accurate
and current information. However, Computer Step and the author shall
not be liable for any loss or damage suffered by readers as a result of
any information contained herein.

Trademarks
All trademarks are acknowledged as belonging to their respective
companies.

Printed and bound in the United Kingdom

ISBN 1-874029-91-1

Contents

1 The basics — **7**

What this book is about	8
Internet basics	10
Introducing Web pages	12
Push technology	14
Netiquette and the spirit of the Web	15
What you need to create Web pages	16
Introducing the Web browser	18
Introducing HTML	19
The Home page	20
Web page components	21
For businesses – Web hot spots	23
Staying legal	24
Getting your site up and running	25

2 Designing for a purpose — **27**

Why set up a Web page?	28
Providing the right information	30
Increasing the value of your pages	31
Establishing a design strategy	32
Considering information design	36
A visitor oriented design approach	37
Technical design requirements	39
Web sites for personal use	41
Small business Web sites	42
Web sites for corporate use	43
The grand design plan	45
Establishing when to stop	46

3 Colour and text considerations — **47**

Colours and colour combinations	48
Working with fonts	49
Creating effective text content	51
Allowing for text-only viewing	52

4   Using graphics   53

Introducing image types   54
Considering image size   57
Establishing colour depth   58
Interlacing images   60
Transparent images   61
Providing impact with imagemaps   62
Using preview images   63
Applying a digital watermark   64

5   The Web page background   65

Background: exotic or plain?   66
Using a black background   68
Creating a picture background   70

6   Including tables and lists   71

The value of tables   72
Some table design options   74
Using tables in forms   76
Presenting information using lists   77

7   Working with frames   79

Why use frames   80
Introducing frame types   81
Applying frames to a Web page   83
Avoiding common pitfalls   84

8   Animating Web pages   85

Using dynamic GIFs   86
Applying flashing components   88
Using Shockwave files   89
Including Java applets   91
JavaScript & JScript components   93
Microsoft's ActiveX   94
Establishing what to animate   95
Some advice on what not to animate   96

Providing for unusual file formats   97
Some example animated Web pages   99

9 Audio on the Web   101

Introducing the basics   102
Using simple voice recordings   104
Including background sounds   106
Using RealAudio   107
Providing music   109
Providing a news service   110
Audioconferencing: the talking Web   111

10 Working with video components   113

Introducing Web video technology   114
Using RealVideo   116
Web video hints and tips   118

11 Creating 3D Web pages   119

Why use 3D on the Web?   120
Virtual Reality Modelling Language   121
Using VRML in business   122

12 Designing the Home page   123

A generic Home page   124
A personal Home page   126
A Home page for doing business   128
Encouraging visitors to return   133
Avoiding dead URL links   135
The email link   136
Creating an electronic signature   137

13 Creating supplementary pages   139

Building a consistent approach   140
Aim to dazzle your visitors   142
Inform, amuse and entertain   144
Making pages interactive   146
Linking back to the Home page   148

Establishing page length 149
Dealing with related Web sites 150

14 Designing Web pages for marketing 151

Establishing your marketing goals 152
The two-step design plan 153
Standing out 154
Advertising on the Web 155
Adding extra value 156
Creating a visitor's experience 158
Using newsgroups 160
Using mailing lists 161
Providing FAQ lists 162

15 Gaining information with online forms 163

Why use a Web form? 164
How Web forms work 165
Web form building blocks 166
Security issues 168
Some design hints and tips 169
Example Web forms 170

16 Designing Web pages to accept orders 171

Providing a secure server 172
Using simple email forms 173
Traditional contact information 174
Designing a Web page order form 175
Setting up shop the Wizard way 177
Getting paid 179

17 Promoting your Web pages 181

Six essential steps 182
Introducing the Search engines 183
Registering your Web presence 185
Monitoring Web page visits 186

Index 187

The basics

Welcome to *Web page design - in easy steps*. The Internet and World Wide Web are here to stay and offer great potential to individuals, companies and organisations. In this chapter, we examine exactly what the Internet and World Wide Web are and what you need to access them. We also introduce some essential points you should know about before designing your Web pages.

Covers

What this book is about | 8

Internet basics | 10

Introducing Web pages | 12

Push technology | 14

Netiquette and the spirit of the Web | 15

What you need to create Web pages | 16

Introducing the Web browser | 18

Introducing HTML | 19

The Home page | 20

Web page components | 21

For businesses – Web hot spots | 23

Staying legal | 24

Getting your Web site up and running | 25

Chapter One

What this book is about

Towards the end of 1996, one estimate put the number of people with access to the Internet at 50 million and rising. That estimate has now risen to over 60 million and is probably already out of date. Clearly, there's something afoot in cyberspace.

This book explains how anyone can benefit from the Internet and World Wide Web by designing effective Web pages. However, to produce rewarding Web pages, you do need to be armed with special knowledge and skills as well as the necessary software tools. This book can help provide the necessary knowledge and skills, whilst the software tools are often freely available (from the Internet), or need not cost much. Here again, hints, tips and information snippets provided in this book can help point you in the right direction. However, to gain most from this book, it's important that you spend some time practising using these tools and trying out your ideas as much as possible.

Throughout this book, I have purposely tried to avoid burdening you with unnecessary jargon. However, sometimes it's unavoidable and for that I apologise. Unfortunately, the fast changing nature of the beast means some jargon inevitably creeps in.

HANDY TIP

I'm biased I know, but take my word for it, this is one handy tip that will pay for itself. You can purchase other *In Easy Steps* books direct from the publishers who are available on 01926 817999, or from most good bookshops and computer superstores.

Computing can be frustrating at times. Designing Web pages is no exception. However, the 'in easy steps' approach is designed to help you avoid taking drastic action

...contd

If you want to find out about the mechanics of creating Web pages, try *HTML in easy steps.*

If you want to learn more about Web browsers, try *Netscape Communicator in easy steps,* or *Internet Explorer 4 in easy steps.*

If you're new to the Internet, why not take a peek at *Internet UK in easy steps.*

Filling in the gaps

Designing and creating Web pages can be a stunningly simple or surprisingly complex business, depending on what you want to do. Perhaps that is one reason why there are so many poorly designed Web sites already running. With the help of this book and other related *In Easy Steps* books, such as those listed in the margin, it's my hope that your Web pages will not be amongst these.

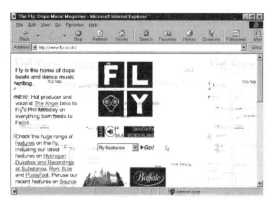

From this example Web page, it's questionable whether the author has made a wise choice of background

Although we aim to cover the design aspects here, unfortunately, there isn't the space to include a great deal about the mechanics of actually producing Web pages or about using popular browsers. However, where possible, the *In Easy Steps* series provides related books which complement others in the series (see Tips in the margin).

I've also assumed you're familiar with Microsoft Windows or the Apple Mac ways of working – that is, using drop-down menus, dialog boxes, icons, buttons, and so on.

Internet basics

The Internet, or 'Net', is a vast collection of interconnected computers spread across the globe providing information on almost any subject imaginable. A visitor using one computer can very quickly and cheaply access information on another computer which may be situated down the road or thousands of miles away: location is irrelevant on the Net!

This can create enormous opportunities and has implications particularly for businesses as well as for individuals. Imagine any customer having access to your shop or front door anywhere around the globe, twenty-four hours a day. If you're in business and are not already 'on the Web', then I suggest the information and guidelines provided in this book could benefit your business – maybe even transform it!

HANDY TIP **For individuals, clubs, companies and organisations involved in providing service support of some kind, a Web site can ensure another support avenue is available for customers or contacts, as well as making savings in traditional service support areas (fewer brochures; lower printing and marketing costs, and so on).**

Here, the designer has produced a clean, uncluttered welcome page which is easy to navigate and includes buttons that are clear and simple to use

Many individuals and businesses who could benefit immensely from Web pages, are still missing out entirely, perhaps mistakenly believing 'it's not for them', or that setting up a Web page is 'beyond' their means. This need not be so. While others – who are 'in the know' have already set up their store in cyberspace – and are poised, if not already, reaping the benefits.

The following page includes information particularly for clubs, businesses and organisations. I invite you to examine the compelling reasons for getting online.

Greater use of the Internet and Web can be good for the environment due to cost savings made in paper, printing, distribution and resulting pollution. Even though electric power consumption increases, many PCs are now 'green-aware', reducing the power used on non-active computers.

For businesses, the Internet can provide access to a vast range of business information; enable users to research existing and new markets, and even provide information about competitors. Use the Web search engines as described in Chapter 17 to find the information you want.

Commercial benefits of a Web site

Already, there are hundreds of thousands of Web pages established. Many of these relate to businesses. So why do they do it. The following list includes some of the benefits a Web site can provide for businesses and organisations:

- There's a global reach; no national boundaries apply

- No premises or similar rental costs are required

- Overheads are low by any similar cost/benefit comparison: Web space is cheap!

- A business can be open 24 hours a day, every day

- When a potential customer is viewing a Web page, the Web page provider has their *total* attention, in contrast to conventional sales avenues. *This should be an important realisation for sales oriented Web sites*

- Sales can be increased cost effectively

- To gain a competitive edge, set up a Web page before your competitors

- Can help reduce marketing costs, especially through the greater use of email to communicate

- By placing representations of corporate printed catalogues on a Web site, fewer conventional printed versions may be needed creating further savings

- Statistics show that many Internet users are affluent: a Web site can therefore provide a direct link to these potentially rich customer profiles

- Different incentives and promotions can be tested quickly and cost effectively

- Certain niche products which can't be sold cost effectively by traditional methods (using retail/mail order for example), may be viable on the Internet because of the low setup and running costs and the powerful global reach

Introducing Web pages

The World Wide Web (WWW) – more commonly known as the Web – is a 'branch' of the Internet and provides access to a vast amount of information through Web pages. Web pages can contain text, images and other graphics, sound, video and other types of animation and are saved as files stored on thousands of computers across the globe. Related separate web pages linked together can be referred to as a Web site. Arguably, the Web is the largest and most complex single information resource across the globe – and it is growing at a breathtaking rate.

You can create HTML using most simple text editors. Some word processors also include 'add-ons' from which you can create the HTML for your Web pages. However usually, it's much easier to use one of the purpose-built applications designed especially for the job.

Simple Web pages can contain only some text and some special codes called tags which determine how this text should appear. The codes used to determine how Web pages and their contents should behave form a simple computer language called HTML (HyperText Markup Language).

HTML is examined in more depth later in this chapter. However, to create Web pages, you don't necessarily need to understand HTML as there are now many graphical 'front end' applications available which let you concentrate on how you want to design your pages rather than how to actually enter the code to make them work. However, to achieve those complex and sometimes tricky special effects, an in-depth knowledge of HTML is valuable.

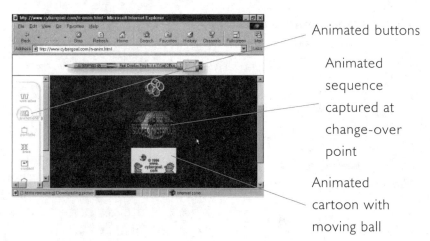

Animated buttons

Animated sequence captured at change-over point

Animated cartoon with moving ball

Using colourful action and attention-grabbing components

To include complex animation-type components in your Web pages, like those in the example shown on the opposite page, can require knowledge and skills using a variety of multimedia-type authoring programs.

There's nothing stopping anyone from obtaining the necessary tools and learning these skills. However, these are powerful programs which take time to learn and to become skilled in using. Therefore, it may be more cost effective to 'buy in' the necessary skills from appropriate contract programmers and graphic artists.

Don't assume the HTML you create will produce the same results on every browser. The browser has most influence on what the visitor actually sees. This is one reason why it's a good idea to test your Web page design on several browsers before publishing to the Web.

Setting up a Web presence – the options

Currently, there are three ways through which you can establish a Web page or Web site:

* Use the Web resources of an Internet Service Provider (Like for example: Demon)

* Establish your own Web hosting infrastructure (have a lot of money ready!)

* Place your Web page(s) in an existing Web mall (like BarclaySquare)

The first option above offers the cheapest and best route for many individuals and companies; it also provides a way of 'testing the waters', without taking on too much risk.

The second option provides the most flexibility, gives you total control but is the most expensive.

The third option – popular in the USA – is gaining ground in the UK also. This approach can be likened to having a shop-in-a-superstore. The Mall (superstore) has hopefully already established a 'position' on the Web with a regular clientele, and so arguably attracts a greater number of potential customers than may be possible using either the first or second option – at least in the short term.

Push technology

The 'traditional' Internet

Normally, if we want to find out about something on the Internet or the Web, but aren't sure where to start, we would probably use the search engines to try and locate our target information. However, often this doesn't isolate what we're looking for effectively enough: we may need to filter out irrelevant information. Also sometimes, listed Web sites may no longer be running or specific Web pages may be missing. Consequently, searching the Web can sometimes be a frustrating and unprofitable experience.

Push technology: the future here now

But there is perhaps a better way starting to emerge called Push technology. Rather than having to search the Web, Push technology promises to reverse this trend and send or 'push' desired information to us. Users subscribe to something that can be likened to channels as in domestic television. We can then decide what sort of information we want – only relevant information is then 'pushed' at regular intervals, without any further action being needed.

REMEMBER

Microsoft's Internet Explorer, from version 4 onwards, is expected to be an important vehicle for promoting Push technology and the change to delivering information in custom-defined 'channels.'

REMEMBER

The type of Internet connection a visitor has, determines the speed and response of their Web connection. An ISDN line or fast company Intranet connection is arguably the best option. However, most of the general public will probably be using 28.8Kb, 33.6Kb or 56Kb modems.

Push technology in action. The Microsoft Internet Explorer v4.0 Active Desktop showing some of the 'Push' Channels available. Hold the mouse pointer over a button to see a brief description

Push technology may bring some teething problems and may possibly become unpopular with some users as some control is lost. However, it is expected to be included in the current versions of Netscape Communicator and Microsoft's Internet Explorer. Although, this technology is new, Internet-related developments can materialise quickly and so Push products could have important consequences for Web page designers. Watch this space!

Netiquette and the spirit of the Web

Netiquette is Internet etiquette, and is therefore simply all about consideration for other online users.

Avoiding the spam

Newsgroups and mailing lists are simply the Internet equivalent of clubs. People who share a common interest or have something to say can post articles, start discussions, seek assistance to solve a problem, and announce something new. But avoid blatant advertising of products and services.

No, we're not talking meat! Spamming is a the term used to describe sending out uninvited email and news clips to vast numbers of users. This sort of activity is usually frowned upon amongst the Internet community. Spamming also helps clog up the Internet for all of us.

Two areas where you should not blatantly advertise products or services are amongst newsgroups and mailing lists. Although by and large, the Internet community implies freedom of spirit and all that goes with it, open advertising in newsgroups and mailing lists is usually not tolerated by those taking part in the forums. However, if this does happen, sometimes warnings are given. Often, if these warnings are ignored, the unpleasant effect of spamming may be used against the inconsiderate advertiser. My advice is to simply consider other users and don't send unsolicited advertisements for any reason.

Share something valuable – and gain!

To avoid breaking netiquette guidelines, when taking part in newsgroups and mailing lists, view the FAQ (Frequently Asked Questions) lists at the start of your sessions.

Some of the most effective and eye-catching sites on the Web work well arguably because their providers are sharing something that has real value. That something could, for example, be some useful information; an offer of free software or try-before-you-buy software; hints and tips on a particular topic; and so on. One reason why the Internet and Web are so popular is the wealth of information anyone can obtain freely or cheaply.

As a Web site provider, you too can also benefit through your Web pages, and create further incentives for people to visit your Web site. If you're hosting a Web information business and you're providing special information, why not provide some (but not all) information in a series. This is reasonable and allows visitors to decide whether it applies to them and get a feel for how they can benefit. For other types of Web sites, you can apply this approach too – and stay in business.

What you need to create Web pages

Those who have already created successful Web pages, will I suspect agree, that much hard work can go into the venture, but that the results can be worth the effort invested. As the Web is a relatively recent phenomenon, understandably, often there are new things to learn. However, the magical ingredient comes from appreciating that your most important work is creative; a product of your own and possibly that of your work colleagues' skills and intuition.

HANDY TIP

Try to aim for a modem speed of at least 33,6Kbps. The new 56Kbps modems are now also available, but do check that your Internet Service Provider supports 56K speeds, and which 56K system they operate (currently, there are two opposing systems).

To create Web pages, you need several things:

- A Web browser installed and set up on a computer or workstation. This will allow you to browse the Web and view your own Web pages

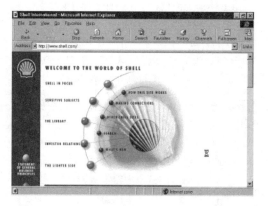

The latest Microsoft Internet Explorer browser, v4.0 (currently free) browser in action viewing one of the beautifully designed Shell Web pages

- An Internet connection either through an Internet Service Provider – an organisation which hosts your Web pages – or if you're going to host your own Web pages, all the kit required to do so (this second option is expensive and requires detailed planning and costing)

- The necessary hardware that will allow you to connect to the Internet. This could be a modem installed and connected to a single computer, or a much faster ISDN line or equivalent often available through a company Internet connection

To view Web pages using Microsoft Windows, you need to have a modem installed and correctly set up to a computer or workstation. Ideally, it should have a minimum specification of 486 33MHz CPU with at least 16Mb of RAM installed.

- You also may need to learn how to enter HTML commands to create the actual Web pages. Alternatively, you could use one of the many dedicated Web page production applications which are now available, making the job arguably much easier. These enable you to concentrate on the content of a Web page rather than all the sometimes tricky commands of HTML. Examples of these products include: shareware programs like *WebExpress* from Microvision Development Inc., or perhaps the more ambitious Microsoft's *FrontPage*

- The last and arguably the most important essential ingredient you need is what this book attempts to address: the design skills necessary to create *effective* Web pages. Key words which relate to this area include things like intuition, first impressions, and the 'feel' or mood a Web site provides. With millions of Web pages already up and running, Web page design skills and associated knowledge are essential to create a successful venture here. Mistakes in the page design can give a totally wrong impression about what you're offering

Once you've created your Web pages, you can publish them to the Web using either:

- The services of your Internet Service Provider

- Or, if you have between £15,000–£30,000+ available, you can set up your own Internet provider server – a powerful dedicated computer designed to serve the PCs and workstations which log on to your Web site

Introducing the Web browser

 When designing your Web pages, it's a good idea to test the results using several Web browsers. As a minimum, use v3 of Netscape Navigator and Microsoft Internet Explorer. Differing browsers can respond differently to various Web page elements. In this way, you can detect and correct potential problems before uploading your Web pages to the WWW.

A Web browser is a dedicated software application which enables you to browse the Web. To view a Web page, once a visitor has entered a Web address, the browser sends a request to the Web server – a powerful computer dedicated to serving Web clients, such as a Web browser. The Web server contains the essential files necessary to display all the Web sites it contains. However, one of the most important things to remember about Web browsers – particularly from a Web page design standpoint – is that different browsers may display the same Web page differently.

Usually, you don't know which browsers your visitors will be using, or the capabilities of their computer systems. This can have implications which affect how you design your Web pages. Older, slower PCs will display a highly graphical Web page containing animated elements slower than a 200MHz Pentium-type PC with 64Mb of RAM. Also remember, any sound elements included in your Web page designs will be lost if visitors don't have a sound card or sound support installed in their computer.

 The way in which a browser is configured also affects how it displays Web pages. For example, some browsers include an option to turn off the automatic display of Java components in a Web page.

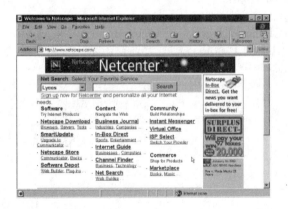

Netscape Navigator (and its latest upgrade, Communicator) still commands a sizeable proportion of the browser market. You can contact the Netscape Web site on http://www.netscape.com

Introducing HTML

The HyperText Markup Language or HTML is really only a set of commands which enable a visitor to 'play' your Web pages. HTML is not really a computer programming language in the pure sense of the word, but is more a collection of special text phrases and 'tags'. Your Web page designs must at some stage be converted to HTML, to enable a PC to understand your Web page commands.

Although this book does not have the space to include in-depth information about HTML, I think you may prefer to gain a better understanding at this stage of what HTML actually is and what it looks like. A basic attribute of a HTML page is the hypertext link or 'hyperlink', which allows a user to click on the link to jump to somewhere else in a document, an entirely different document, or somewhere else on the Web. A hypertext link can be a text- or graphics-based.

To get a better idea of what HTML looks like, often a command is available in the browser which allows you to view the 'source' code, as shown in the example below.

HANDY TIP **If you don't like the look of HTML, there's another way. Software is available which allows you to create Web pages without having to know much about HTML. For example, check out *FrontPage* from Microsoft or *WebExpress* from Microvision Inc.**

HANDY TIP **Some well known applications like WordPerfect, PageMaker, CorelDraw, and Microsoft Office provide tools from which you can easily convert standard documents to HTML format.**

The Home page

Home page design really starts with defining why you want to set up a Web page, and can benefit from a little self analysis. Why? Because a Home or Index page is like your front door: it's the first thing visitors will see when they log onto your Web site, and as such is arguably the most important part of any Web site.

If you include a font in a Web page which is not present on a visitor's computer, their Web browser will try to match the missing font with the nearest available. This can result in Web pages appearing very different from what the designer intended. At worst, a completely muddled display can result.

It's not difficult to create a Web page: many tools are available to help make the job easier. The greater challenge however, is to create an effective and successful Web page and one that works well for you.

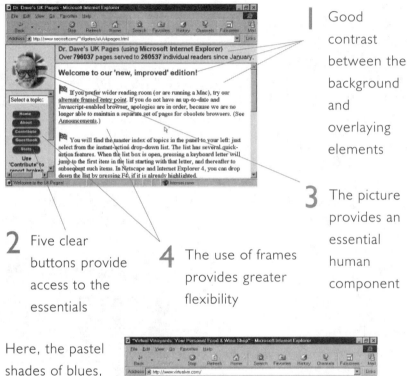

Good contrast between the background and overlaying elements

2 Five clear buttons provide access to the essentials

3 The picture provides an essential human component

4 The use of frames provides greater flexibility

Here, the pastel shades of blues, greens, magentas, and light orange combined with soft-edged graphics, help put over a relaxing atmosphere

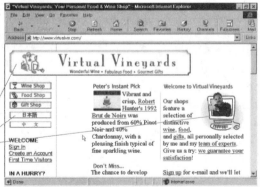

Web page components

If you want people to respond to your Web page, it's a good idea to include the MAILTO command in addition to traditional contact information. In HTML, MAILTO enables a visitor to send an email quickly and easily to the email address you specify.

Before becoming too involved designing Web pages, make sure that you're familiar with using a Web browser. To check your designs later, you may want to view them ideally in several browsers and across several different platforms (Windows, Mac, UNIX workstation, etc.).

A Web page can include many components or building blocks. For example:

- Page titles

- Text headings and main text content

- Buttons and icons: navigational signposts

- Tables: to provide a neat row and column format or to help break up the predictable structure of a Web page

- Lists: help identify essential points in the text

- Horizontal line separators

- Simple and complex images

- Frames: can help provide more flexibility and an easier navigation structure for your Web pages

- Animation: components which provide movement and action can transform a Web page

- Sound buttons: providing access to sound clips, interviews and music extracts

- 3D effects

The use of high quality graphics and careful consideration of the design, is evident in this Microsoft Web page

Design planning for a wide range of visitors

Two of the most basic requirements necessary to achieve effective Web page design, include:

- The ability to create pages that are visually interesting

- Pages which will look good even when viewed using perhaps older, less powerful Web browsers

REMEMBER

Netscape Navigator/ Communicator and Microsoft Internet Explorer users don't need to insert 'http://' when entering a Web address. An address starting with 'www' is sufficient.

Meeting the previous two conditions can be quite challenging. Sometimes, it's easy to assume that the entire planet uses only two types of Web browsers: either Netscape Navigator/Communicator or Microsoft Internet Explorer. However, of course this is not so. Several other well known browsers across the globe command a loyal following. Therefore, it's a good idea to keep this in mind when considering your page designs; in fact, depending on the profile of your target audience, this fact may become an important yardstick.

Browsers from sources other than Microsoft & Netscape are available

For businesses – Web hot spots

Here's a list of business areas that are currently popular on the Internet – and remember that includes the Web:

- Computer software
- Computer hardware
- Books
- Music
- Videos and movies
- Travel services
- Financial services
- Insurance
- Brokerage services
- Banks
- Theatre, concerts and plays
- Jewellery
- Sunglasses
- Shoes
- Special, unique or unusual products

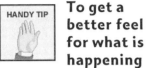

To get a better feel for what is happening on the Internet in terms of business opportunities, try pointing your Web browser at the following Web sites where a wealth of free information is usually available: http:// www.gartner.com and: http:// www.forrester.com

Most businesses have the potential to be marketed on the Web, although some, by their nature are more likely to be more successful than others.

Some firms are already making money using their Web sites, either through making savings elsewhere or by making available entirely new sales channels. However, currently for most businesses, use of the Web can:

- Provide a new answer to the often recurring theme of how to improve customer services whilst saving money
- Show how to widen the corporate presence still further but cost effectively

Page 11 of this chapter examines the obvious benefits to businesses and organisations in more depth.

Staying legal

From a legal standpoint, setting up a Web page is relatively new territory. You need to be careful, whether you're creating a personal, club, small business or corporate Web site. Companies and organisations need to consider their corporate policies and the legalities of putting information on a Web site. For example, a company might need to re-examine whether the aspect of what is 'their' information, and the implications of including such information if it is truly not 'owned' by the company.

 If you decide to include links to other Web sites on your Web pages, it pays to check out those sources. Recent litigation examples show that Web sites hosting links to companies already being sued, can themselves become embroiled in the legal action, simply for hosting a Web site link.

Checking the need for permits

If you're starting a Web-based business from new, remember, you may still need to purchase relevant permits, so check into these aspects well in advance. For companies and organisations, it may be wise to seek advice from a lawyer specialising in Internet business practices.

Acknowledging copyright

Everything on the Web is 'owned' by somebody. Although some may consider information provided on the Internet is 'public domain', if you 'borrow' components from other Web pages, at least provide an acknowledgement of the owner's work. To ensure complete safety from the threat of litigation, simply don't use other people's materials unless you have written permission to do so. This is understandable and reasonable:

 Whoever you are, if you want to protect and lay claim to 'your' work included on a Web page, at least include a dated copyright notice such as: '© 1998. All rights reserved.'

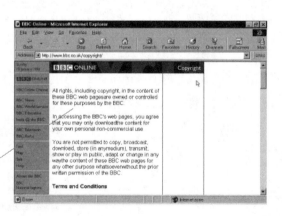

no one likes to have their hard work ripped off by someone else to benefit without at least correct recognition being given.

Getting your site up and running

Once you're happy with the design of your Web pages, you can upload them to the Web using any of the following methods:

- Set up your own dedicated Web server – this is a fast, powerful computer with equally fast Internet access – and also install and set up all the necessary communications software and protocols. This is a serious option and one which can cost many thousands of pounds to set up and maintain

- The second option which most people choose, is to upload your Web pages to your chosen Internet Service Provider. Often, ISPs provide a few megabytes of Web space available to each member as part of their package. For example, the author uses BT Internet and they provide 5Mb free Web space with their *Plan Unlimited* offering

- A third option is to buy Web space from an existing Web mall. A mall, in this context, is simply any organisation which has already established a prominent presence and which hosts other Web site providers. It can be likened to having a shop in a supermarket: the supermarket draws the crowds, and in-store shop benefits from the traffic flow – for a fee

 HANDY TIP

If you're using a 56Kbps modem to connect to the Internet, yet the actual speed of access appears not to be more than about 26Kbps, try contacting your telephone line supply company. Tell them you're using the line for Internet access: sometimes, 'line cleaning' work can improve connection speeds.

Once your Web site is active, usually you can upload any changes or updates whenever you want, and most ISPs can provide further Web space if you need it – but do compare prices if you decide to exercise this option: the Web is developing at a breathtaking pace and with competition becoming ever more fierce, new and better deals are emerging all the time.

Don't under-estimate the importance of having an appropriate Web address. This has real value and can be included in traditional advertising media like brochures, advertisements, and so on.

Some businesses have similar-sounding names. As domain names are allocated on a first-come, first-served basis, another similar-sounding business or organisation could register their domain name before you. In which case, you would have to think of some other URL. With some businesses, this could result in significant lost revenues.

Your email address and domain name

Your email address says a lot about you – or if you're in business – your company or organisation. In fact, if you're developing a business oriented Web site, meaningful email and Web addresses are essential if you're to be taken seriously. Remember, on the Web, people make assumptions by what they see or hear. On the Internet, your email and Web addresses often provide the first link in this communications chain.

For example, consider the following imaginary email addresses, referring to our imaginary John Smith, who is the MD for our imaginary company, Sheldon Plastics. Of the three, which do you think provides a better image?

john_smith@compuserve.com

john_smith@aol.com

john_smith@SheldonPlastics.co.uk

My own choice would be the third option: it's arguably more meaningful and more professional. Now let's link in the Home or Index Web page address. Remember, every Web site has its own address in the form of a URL. Now, if you wanted to use the following URL:

http://www.SheldonPlastics.co.uk

Providing no one else was already using that address, you could protect your URL – otherwise known as a domain – by registering this as your domain name. Domain names are assigned and registered on a first-come, first-served basis, so in our imaginary example, as John Smith is in business, it would be wise of him to establish a domain name as soon as possible – even well before starting his Web page design.

Most Internet Service Providers can arrange to register your domain name. As a rough guide, the one-off cost is currently approximately £100–£150 plus a further monthly or annual maintenance fee. Contact your ISP for details.

Chapter Two

Designing for a purpose

One of the most basic aspects we should remember when designing Web pages is the importance of structured planning right from the start. Planning can be broken down into key components. This chapter tackles these issues for individuals, companies and organisations, both small and large.

Covers

Why set up a Web page? | 28

Providing the right information | 30

Increasing the value of your pages | 31

Establishing a design strategy | 32

Considering information design | 36

A visitor oriented design approach | 37

Technical design requirements | 39

Web sites for personal use | 41

Small business Web sites | 42

Web sites for corporate use | 43

The grand design plan | 45

Establishing when to stop | 46

Why set up a Web page?

The Internet and the World Wide Web are two of the most hyped buzz-words of the 1990s. There's good reason for this to be so. The Web still has enormous potential. When asked, people can give varying reasons for wanting to set up a Web site – including the desire simply to 'have a presence on the Internet'. However, most interpretations can be grouped under one or more of the following categories:

•   To advertise an interest, product or service

•   To provide information

•   To enable transactions to take place

 The Internet is like a new, ungoverned territory. For individuals and especially businesses, there are new risks as well as enormous opportunities. Identify clearly why you want a Web site and then weigh the benefits against the risks.

Through a Web page, email provides you with another method of dialogue, and can ensure you have access to a new, direct low cost communications channel to your visitors. Remember also, email can be received almost instantly, so it can be considered as a 'quick results' tool, much quicker than conventional mail. We'll look at email in more depth later.

Three steps to help make it work

To help ensure a Web page is effective, consider the following guidelines:

1   The most important point to consider is that it should have a *clearly defined purpose*. Often, this can be defined better by putting pen to paper and noting down your reasons for wanting to create your Web page(s)

2   Secondly, you should have *something interesting to say, to portray or discuss*. The more unique, useful, attractive, or compelling your subject matter is, the better

3   Your third aim should be to try and include aspects on your Web pages that will encourage and urge visitors to *want to return*. The harsh reality is that most people are unlikely to revisit boring or irrelevant sites

For businesses: establishing primary objectives

Consider the three primary objectives of any business-oriented Web page(s):

- To create more sales from existing customers

- Create new sales orders from entirely new customers

- Reduce the cost of running the business generally

To achieve all three is the pinnacle objective, but is not so easy. Achieving one of the conditions above should benefit a business. Achieving two should create more sales. Fulfilling all three objectives should dramatically increase profits.

Forrester Research suggest most businesses are online in an attempt to lead the way. Fewer are doing so because their customers are also online. Fewer still, do so, simply to keep up with the others, and the lowest proportion are on the Web simply to experiment with the idea.

Advertising – a primary aim

Currently, most Web sites are set up, at least initially, to advertise. Advertising on the Web is usually much cheaper than using traditional media like brochures, magazines and newspapers. However, often these types of Web sites may be set up to supplement, rather than to replace, conventional advertising methods. Consider the following two important points:

- Advertising-oriented Web sites are usually the easiest to set up as no complex routines are needed to deal with transactions

- However, to achieve the desired effect, it's vital for this kind of Web site to appear interesting or striking, and to contain elements that encourage and compel visitors to return

Providing the right information

The type of Web site you're setting up really determines the structure and therefore affects the sort of information you'll provide. We may set up a Web site to:

Here's a statistic to consider: Forrester Research suggest the Internet could be processing £201 billion pounds globally by the year 2002, with most of this going to a few clearly defined manufacturers and specific industrial markets.

- Promote hobbies, special interests, and so on

- Benefit a company or organisation

- Provide a forum for open discussion

- Deliver customer support services

Information-providing Web pages

Some Web sites may contain thousands of pages; others just a few. The more information you provide in a Web site, the more important it is for that information to be easily accessible by your audience. Although, it's possible to use varying and increasingly innovative methods to meet this need, keeping the system simple and direct may often offer the best course of action to follow.

When considering what to include in a Web page, usually many choices emerge. However, why not try to put yourself in the place of a visitor and ask what they would want. Establish what they might look for. Make a short list, then leave out anything else not essential.

Information-seeking visitors also want quick access. However, most visitors are reasonable people and may be prepared to periodically put up with some discreet advertising or attempts to sell a product or service. But if this is overdone and too much 'hoop jumping' is felt by visitor, then the reverse is probably true. Therefore, do consider this approach carefully: this may be one of the fastest ways to lose a customer.

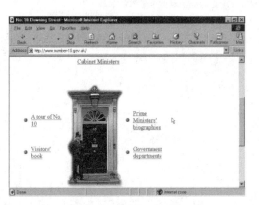

The Number 10 Downing Street Web site presents a clean, uncluttered opening page with a few clear options centred around a world-renowned brand image, the front door to No 10

Increasing the value of your pages

 Although words provide the 'glue' which holds everything together, the Web is essentially a graphical medium. Therefore, try to make a Web page colourful, vibrant and lively.

 Once you've stimulated visitors to visit your Web pages, to maintain interest, update the pages regularly; also, let visitors know when you'll be doing this.

 Some of the best Web sites follow a simple design theme, with technologically exotic components kept to a minimum. In a highly cluttered Web, open space often stands out.

People appreciate being considered! Sometimes, results reflecting this can be better achieved by stressing what you leave out rather than what you decide to include in your Web pages.

There's a great tendency now on many Web sites to include as much action, animation, electronic tricks, flashing logos, graphics or icons as possible. However, complex content may not always be perceived as 'interesting'. When devising your Web page structure, unless you have a specific need to surprise readers, often it's better to consider carefully how much animation or moving elements you include in mainly text-based Web pages. Ill-considered flashing and moving elements and inappropriate background sounds can confuse and interfere with readers' ability to absorb the main message of the page.

With download times for Web pages still relatively slow even with the fastest 56 Kbps modems, I suggest your audience will thank you for it and probably have good cause to remember your 'clean, uncluttered site.' One good benchmark to aim for is to try and ensure the essential content of your Home page is fully downloaded within about 25 seconds using a 28.8 Kbps modem, sooner if possible. Saving several seconds by applying careful design techniques is always worthwhile. Remember, every second counts!

Animated Web pages however, provide a powerful and entertaining accompaniment – when presented carefully and appropriately. These aspects are examined in more detail in Chapters 8, 9, 10, and 11.

Including image text markers

For every instance in which you provide an image on a Web page, make sure you include the necessary HTML code to provide a text equivalent. Why? Because some visitors disable the graphics capabilities of their browsers to reduce the page download time. Without text markers for the graphics, such a Web page may not make much sense.

Establishing a design strategy

To create effective Web pages, you need to complete two main tasks:

- Create working HTML code that meets the current HTML standard

- Devise designs that are interesting, attractive and which are 'tuned' to the interests of your visitors

When planning a design, some people find it useful to put pen to paper before using the HTML software. You could try drawing a flowchart illustrating which Web pages you want displayed and in which sequence.

Strong branding logically placed and prominently displayed

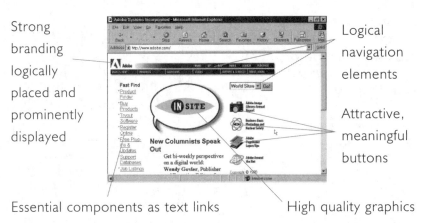

Logical navigation elements

Attractive, meaningful buttons

Essential components as text links

High quality graphics

You can gain ideas about how to design your Web pages by seeing how other, similar Web sites appear. You can scan magazines and newspapers containing Web site reviews, then go online and check them out. If you're in business, check out the competition and consider the benefits and drawbacks of their style of Web presence.

Some design pointers

Several aspects can affect the way you can design your Web pages. You could consider:

- Your URL or Web page address can be an important marketing aid. When devising it, try to think of how your visitors will try to locate you

- Is the Web page attractive? Does it immediately make an impression on the first visit?

- Carefully focus design aspects towards the target audience, to ensure they can quickly identify with what you're saying or offering

- From the outset, it's a good idea to set up a system to log all email addresses of those who visit your site, and then build on it. For example, for a business: your email contacts could represent hot prospects

When preparing your graphics in conversion programs like Paint Shop Pro and Adobe Photoshop, you may be given a choice of palettes. If possible, choose Adaptive or Optimized at the conversion stage to obtain a closer match as possible to the original.

A Web page can be compared to a presentation. If your Web pages are dealing with a particularly complex subject matter, why not present your case better by providing information in bit-sized chunks. Use (active) space to provide plenty of 'breathing space'.

Avoiding the mistakes of others

There are many sources of research on the Internet relating to the Internet and World Wide Web. Often, the results shows where mistakes have been made. You can benefit from these errors by learning more about this subject. For example, recent research has shown:

- Visitors become irritated when trying to navigate through a poorly designed Web site

- Whilst examining a Web page, visitors don't like to have to scroll

- Visitors are not keen to read what they consider to be unnecessary material. Often, this type of content is simply skipped

Some suggested 'golden rules'

- If your Web site is essentially acting as an information resource, text and fast-loading graphics should dictate your design strategy. In this event, it's probably a good idea to limit the use of special animation effects like Shockwave and Java content

- If your Web site is primarily aimed at entertaining or advertising, Shockwave- and Java-type animations will probably enhance your presentation. However, do consider your visitors: try to define the level of computer equipment they're likely to be using, then modify your designs to match

- Never forget the three most important reasons why visitors may be 'turned off' a Web site:

  - When it's boring

  - If it takes too long to load

  - Visitors become confused while trying to use it

Dealing with different Web browsers

From a visitor's perspective, Web access is provided through their browser and how it's set up. Knowing the types of browsers commonly used by visitors can affect how you design your pages. At an early stage in the design process therefore, it's a good idea to remember that many of your visitors may be connecting to your site using any one of the following types of browsers:

- PC-based, like Netscape Navigator/Communicator or Microsoft's Internet Explorer

- Apple Mac-based

- Commodore Amiga-type

- UNIX-based, or

- A simple text-based terminal with no graphics display capability (although I suspect, not many users still prefer these)

Getting to know your visitors can be an ongoing concern even after your Web pages are active. You can create email forms and ask visitors to complete brief questionnaires about themselves continually building dynamic profiles. Correct, reliable and up-to-date information has real value.

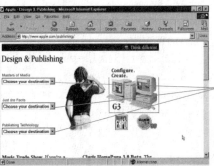

The Apple Mac Web site demonstrates a rich background in graphical imagery and design skills and provides quick easy access to wide range of information

Here, Apple have made good use of the power of black-to-white and yellow-to-black colour contrast

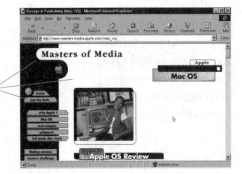

Profiling your expected visitors

Before you start to design your Web pages, try to:

HANDY TIP **In a 'busy' Web page, if you want to draw attention to a brief span of text, you could consider using the <MARQUEE> tag in HTML. Browsers that support this feature will then scroll text across the screen as defined by the HTML parameters.**

(1) Understand who your visitors are and what type of computer technology they're likely to be using. For example:

- Decide on a minimum specification PC, say 486 processor

- Which operating systems do you think they're using

- If possible, try to establish or make a calculated guess how many have sound cards installed

- What is the range and power of video cards used

- Which fonts are commonly available

- And so on

HANDY TIP **Computers can often present a cold, uncaring face. Why not try to bring some warmth to a Web page by maximising the human element where you can. Relate your message using content that is familiar to people everywhere, using sights, sounds, thoughts and feelings.**

(2) Then you can decide the level of complexity you're going to use in your Web page design, making sure that it matches as closely as possible to that of your visitors profile in (1) above

Carrying out the exercise above may seem tedious and difficult. However, it's sometimes amazing what you can find out by putting pen to paper, noting down what you already know and applying some simple telemarketing techniques. The essential aim of this exercise is to avoid upsetting potential visitors. This kind of information can also help you to fine-tune your Web page design; provide the best you can for your visitors and maintain your Web site better once it is up and running.

Considering information design

Information design is really about establishing what to include and what to omit from a Web page, and as such is a crucial element in the design process. Consider the following guidelines:

Often, the most attractive and appealing Web pages have benefited by the skills of professional Web page designers and graphic artists. These skills cost money, but the results can set your site apart from the crowd.

- Each Web page in your series has a distinct purpose and a central message; keep this in mind when designing your pages

- Create a logical hierarchy in the display of information. This presents an obvious and easy-to-understand at-a-glance structure

- Try to make sure a page is not too 'busy', or contains several prominent elements which fight for the prime attention. Keep to one focus on each page if possible

- Balance page components by subtle use of strong and weak colours as well as physical size and placement

Your Web page can become an electronic brochure

Web pages are similar in some ways to brochures: both can advertise products and services and both can provide information. Yet a Web page can go much further, providing interactive components, including movement and action and allowing orders to be taken quickly.

For some smaller business-oriented Web pages, sometimes simple is best – especially in the payments area. If a credit card call back system works profitably for you, then seriously question why you should spend more time and money trying to change it.

Advertising: comparing magazines with the Web

From a Web page design aspect, it's a good idea to consider carefully how you're going to design a Web advertisement. If a printed version already exists, in say printed magazine form, don't assume that the printed advert can simply be used on a Web page. The content and layout may need to be redesigned to be presented properly on a Web page.

As Web pages are displayed using a display monitor, different presentation requirements are required: for example, results of research shows that most readers usually find reading from a screen more difficult than reading from paper. Many users also wear glasses or contact lenses, so further strain on the eyes will not enrich their Web experiences.

A visitor oriented design approach

 Try to make sure each of your Web pages fully loads within about 25 seconds using a 28.8Kbps modem. Many visitors may start to lose patience after that time lapse and may not bother to revisit your site.

Generally, Web page visitors want results fast; they don't want to spend unnecessary time dawdling online. Web page designers therefore, would do well to design quick, simple and attractive Web pages that include at least two of these three traits. Three further pointers affect Web page design, consider:

- What makes up each page

- The basic structure – is it clear and quick to use?

- How the Web page is delivered to your readers

Focusing on visitors' needs

It's a good idea to make sure visitors know what to expect when they reach your Home or Index page (the first page in your system). If your visitors expect to find information on a specific page, but only find advertising, they may become irritated and start to lose faith in your pages.

Many aspects can affect how you identify your visitors, including the following:

 To save on download time, some visitors may disable graphics display in their browsers. This is why it's important to always include text labels 'behind' graphic and other non-text elements. In this event, if text labels are not included, visitors would not be able to make sense of the Web page. Fortunately, you can easily set this up in HTML.

- Their approximate age? The range of jobs they perform. Are they young or more mature? Younger visitors might prefer a dynamic, highly colourful approach, whereas perhaps professional management consultants, for example, might identify better with a more subtle, corporate feel

- Where do they live? What language do they speak? And so on. Some would argue English is becoming an accepted international language, but even the English language has variations: American, Canadian, International, and British; So this may highlight possible spelling oddities. Colours and combinations of colours can also have special meaning in some cultures

- Is their equipment capable of displaying your Web pages fully? You can avoid this problem by including a simple text equivalent for every graphic or other non-text element

For text headings, to provide contrast and clarity, consider using a non-serif-type font, like Arial, Verdana or Lucida Sans. Remember, non-serif fonts don't have tails on the edges of letters.

For the main body text in a Web page, consider using a serif typeface – that is one in which the edges of letters have tails. Serif fonts are generally easier to read at smaller sizes, especially on a computer monitor.

Some logo designs may include text content that may appear too small on a display monitor, and so not all logos may be appropriate to use on a Web page.

Creating a consistent style

From the Home page onwards, it's a good idea to try and create a similar style of presentation across all the pages in your Web site. If icons are used to act as buttons/ hyperlinks, you could repeat the usage of appropriate icons from this batch or create others which are obviously of the same style.

If you're designing a Web site for a company or organisation which uses a logo on conventional marketing materials, then inserting the logo on each page helps carry over the familiar structure and branding as well as radically increasing the amount of exposure the logo would otherwise receive (see the Beware note in the margin of this page).

By using familiar components, like the same toolbars, fonts, tables, and following the same information delivery plan across the pages, visitors know what to expect, and so this helps them absorb information more easily.

Creating consistency between multiple authors

If you're the only person involved in creating your Web pages, you can let your creative flair blossom. However, if several people become involved in designing a Web site, often it's a good idea at the outset to establish a set style to use, to ensure all the pages 'fit' together. This stylesheet template could establish such things as:

- Text sizes and font styles for different levels of headings (page title, 1st level head, 2nd level, etc.)

- Logo size and positioning

- Button icons: style, size and positioning

- Page background

- Frames layout

- And so on

Technical design requirements

Meeting the HTML standard

Currently, the HyperText Markup Language (HTML) is used to create working Web pages. Since HTML developed several years ago, it has gone through several revisions and updates, from HTML version 1, through to versions 2 to version 3.2 and the current version 4.

When designing your Web pages, it's important to ensure they meet the current HTML standard. You can find out what the current HTML version is by pointing your browser to the World Wide Web Consortium (W3C) Web site. The W3C set the HTML standards and are available at :http://www.w3.org/

Wizards can do the bulk of Web page creation for you. Simply answer some basic questions and the software does the rest. You can then make final adjustments manually. Microsoft *FrontPage* is one well known wizard-driven application.

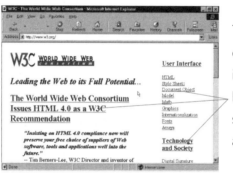

The W3C Web pages are designed for quick access to information using lots of hyperlinks. The design is simple, is mainly text-based and is well laid out

The types of pages that can make up a Web site

Any Web site can be made up of three types of Web pages:

- The Home page: this is often the first page which a visitor sees (sometimes a Welcome page precedes this)

- Intermediate pages: these are the pages which are 'the next level down' immediately accessible from the Home page. Usually, there's a link back to the Home page from each of these intermediate pages

- Content pages: these contain subject details and are usually accessible from Intermediate pages. Often, Content pages may also include a link back to the Home page in addition to other relevant links

To make the job of Web page design easier, you can purchase Web page components like buttons, icons, backgrounds, and clip art especially prepared for use in Web pages. But do consider clip art components carefully: sometimes they may not really produce the desired effect.

Dealing with images – a special case

Computers can have all sorts of specifications; some of your visitors may have the latest, super fast PCs, others may be surfing the Internet with quite old machines. Considering the bewildering range of different computer configurations possible, we could be forgiven for thinking that it's impossible to design Web pages that will display correctly on every browser/PC combination. That may be so, however, I can offer some advice which will ensure that most visitors will be able to display your graphics once they've been prepared for use on the Web.

The most important aspect is related to the video capability of a visitor's computer. Most up-to-date PCs can provide a video resolution of 1600 x 1200 pixels using 24-bit colour (see Chapter 4, page 58 for more information about bit-colour depth). Nevertheless, this can be considered a high specification; many computer owners use 800 x 600 at 256 colours, 16-bit, or 24-bit colour depth.

The majority of modern PCs are probably capable of displaying a 640 x 480 resolution at 256 colours, so to ensure *maximum* compatibility with your visitors computers, you could design your pages to meet this criteria. The next best option is to stick with 800 x 600, which is arguably the most common resolution used today.

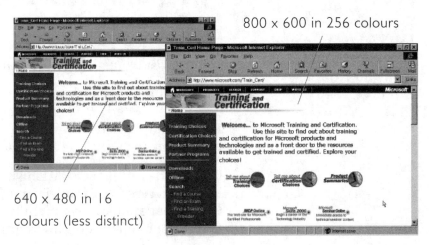

800 x 600 in 256 colours

640 x 480 in 16 colours (less distinct)

Web sites for personal use

Web sites are not just for companies and organisations. In fact some of the best Web pages have been developed by individuals who want to promote their hobby or interest and connect with other like minded individuals. In this way, the Web can produce and stimulate the development of many smaller communities.

Providing a Web page, may not cost you anything if you already have an email account. It's possible that your Internet Service Provider may already include some free Web space for you to use should you choose to. Speak to your ISP for details.

Advice offered on this and the following few pages can equally apply to creating club oriented Web pages.

Adopt a theme

When designing a personal Web site, although visitors will probably expect you to talk about yourself, often, the last thing they want to read is lots of egocentric 'I' words. One way to avoid this situation is to design your Web pages around a theme. For example, this could be the place where you live, a keen hobby or interest. In this way, you can captivate visitors by introducing the things that interest you before mentioning something about yourself.

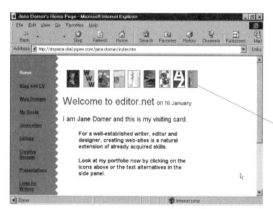

This writer centres her Web pages on communications and design skills. Valuable background inform-ation is also provided. Buttons effectively link to the key parts of her Web site

Creating a twenty-four hour online c.v.

In a personal Web site, you can let your creative flair blossom. In fact, some individuals use a personal Web site as a kind of curriculum vitae. Many others at least include their c.v. as one of their Web pages. An online c.v. can provide a powerful demonstration of your abilities and imagination. If you include a photograph, choose one that put's over warmth. If the career approach is foremost in your mind, you could always discuss this aspect with a professional photographer to help get the best results.

Small business Web sites

In the business world, arguably, those who have most to gain from hosting a Web site are small businesses. A Web site is probably the only way in which small businesses can present their products and services on the same level as the larger companies and organisations. A Web site for a tiny business can project an image as good as, or better than, an international company: the key is the page design.

For businesses especially, plan your Web site venture seriously. According to recent statistics from Gartner Group research, 80% of Web retail ventures fail within the first year.

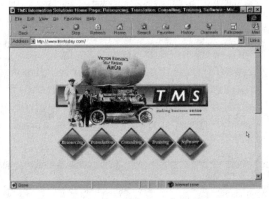

The excellent design of this company Home page demonstrates careful consideration with quality aspects clearly shown

The Internet and the Web are causing a lot of commercial interest. To-date in the UK, almost 100,000 businesses of all sizes have set up shop on the Internet in a variety of ways.

Web transactions

If you want to deal with money on your Web site, extra design input is required in addition to further HTML coding. Also, your Internet Service Provider must be able to handle online forms. Different providers use different scripts to handle this kind of information so discuss these aspects with them at an early stage.

If you're at the stage of finding an Internet Service Provider or changing to another one, the ability to handle online transactions must be established if you want to handle Web transactions through your Web pages.

As transaction-type Web pages involve considerably more technical and design input, they can cost more to develop. However, there's no reason why any small business cannot deal with basic Web transactions (see Chapter 16).

Web sites for corporate use

Setting up a Web site to take orders can be both a benefit and a shock – if you're not ready for it. Web businesses are open to a global market 24 hours a day, 7 days a week, all throughout the year. Ask yourself truly: 'Can the business handle this level of exposure?'

For large corporate users, considering setting up a Web site is a particularly important step. If you host the entire operation yourself, costs can be high: the Gartner Research Group suggest the annual running costs could be as high as 5–6 times the start-up cost.

Setting up a corporate Web site can be the most complex of all as many issues may be involved. For example, many companies have a clearly defined policy regarding the use of the logo and other corporate graphic styles. Therefore, this and other such aspects should be considered early in your Web site design as part of an overall design plan.

Also, there's the aspect of security; you need to be sure that access to your Web site doesn't provide a weak link to the often priceless information within your company. Costs are therefore unavoidably high for setting up a corporate Web site. The benefits can also be enormous or trivial. Arguably, this depends largely on the seriousness of planning and approach. However, currently, many corporates want a Web site simply because their clients and suppliers already have one or are currently setting one up.

Allowing for special pages

Some larger corporate Web sites may require special pages such as those below:

- A page for logging in: this may involve user names, ID numbers and passwords

- Some corporate sites include their own search facilities. Therefore, several types of pages providing access to a local Help search engine may also be required

- User registration purposes: visitors may need to register. This type of Web page may be included in the first point above or may be kept separate

- Pages to meet legal requirements, disclaimers, assertion of copyright, and so on

Carrying out transactions on the Web

When considering the business of Web transactions, the same advice as provided on the opposite page for small businesses also applies to corporates. However, arguably the demands and risks are greater so you need to be sure everything works correctly.

The World Wide Web is part of a fairly new landscape. In this ungoverned land, the rules are hazy at best. For any business wanting to create a Web presence, the watchword is: 'To plan ahead in detail and to be careful.'

For established businesses thinking of providing a Web presence, consider employing experts to create a new Web brand image. Branding is often considered to be an essential component of any successful Net-business.

A Web site reflects the company as a whole. A 'bad' Web site can undo years of previous successes.

The Net-successful: one example

Clearly, money can be made on the Web, but arguably, it's not suitable for every business. Also, the product, branding, and the strategy have to be right from the start.

Let's take a brief look at one company that has been hailed by many as an icon for successful trading on the Internet: Dell computers. Currently, Dell takes orders online for more than two million PCs each day. Their Web store daily provides £1.25 million in sales. By any comparison, that's impressive. However, when we look a little closer, we can see that, arguably Dell's position is more unusual than most on the Web. One could say, their online store could easily be set up. Consider the following points:

- Before starting up a Web presence, they already had an impressive IT infrastructure established

- Their business empire already traded on a global scale

- They had been dealing directly with the public for some time before setting up their online presence

- The techniques, and to a certain extent, the experience, were already established, at least in part

So for Dell, perhaps we could say the Internet and Web represented a natural progression, an evolutionary development, rather than a completely new venture.

These same arguments can perhaps apply to many other types of companies and organisations. For example, banks and retail stores – especially those selling computer software, books or music products. Perhaps this is one reason why many businesses in these categories have made successful transitions to the Web and appear to be promoting themselves well on the Internet.

The point is that any individual, club, business or organisation can make true assessments of strengths, weaknesses, opportunities and threats (SWOT test) in relation to providing a possible presence on the Web.

The grand design plan

How off-screen planning can benefit your design

Before setting to work with HTML or a dedicated Web page design software application, why not sit down with pencil and paper and note down your initial ideas. In this way, you can create a logical opening structure and try out different approaches gathering your thoughts better: using Web page software on its own is not necessarily the best way to do this.

Another potentially useful way to develop ideas for your Web site is to brainstorm with friends or colleagues. Each can write down initial thoughts – however wacky – then collectively discuss ideas. Finally, build a plan from the results.

You could draft the opening Web page, trying to keep this appropriate to your visitors and as inviting as possible, but simple. Avoid including too many choices. You could do this by keeping to the 7–10 options rule limit. These could be buttons, icons, individual parts of a larger image, or simply text components.

Make a checklist to log your progress

Putting Web pages together effectively involves a surprising variety of skills. It's easy therefore to make simple errors in spelling; create incorrect grammar; incorrect or dead URLs, and so on. To avoid this, try carrying out the following routine:

Once your Web design is complete, don't upload it to the Web until you've thoroughly tested it's response using several browsers ideally. To maintain credibility, it's important to test and re-test every aspect before publishing to the Web.

1　When your Web pages are almost complete, it's a good idea to create a checklist to prevent these 'howlers' getting through

2　Then to rigidly check all the Web pages only for one type of fault in the list at a time. If you see other mistakes while checking for one type of fault, resist the temptation to be swayed: you'll pick up those faults later

3　Here's an idea of what to check: spelling, grammar, punctuation, layout, dead URL links, style consistency, all links, download times – graphics especially, and animation elements

Establishing when to stop

No one should presume to tell you when your Web page design is 'right', only you as the designer really knows that. But you can reach a stage beyond which any further contribution you make doesn't improve the result, and can possibly ruin what was originally a 'good' design.

Lessons from the artists

Sometimes the desire to create something special can lead to adding complex cutting-edge features to a Web page. This may be fine, but if ill-considered, can result in a one-browser-only Web page – this would not be good for business. Test drive such designs with multiple browsers to prevent this problem occurring.

How often as children, have many of us created a drawing or painting of which we're proud, only to become so excited that we try to 'make it a little better.' By the time we realise the mistake, it's too late – the picture is spoiled. And as grownups, many professional artists providing drawing and painting workshops press home the point to their students: 'Don't overdo it', 'Know when to stop'; some even say: 'When you think the drawing is almost complete, that's the time to stop!'

A Web page is essentially a graphical medium, so this kind of advice can be relevant here too. As we design our pages, it's easy to become so absorbed and to enjoy the business of creating Web pages, that we can sometimes lose sight of the real goal, namely: to create an attractive, usable and interesting offering which people will want to revisit again and again.

Harnessing the power of active space

Space has power! Yes, even empty areas of a Web page can deliver a powerful message in their own right. Considered use of empty space is not really empty at all: it's active. This 'active space' adds to the overall offering. So many Web pages now are filled with pointless 'clutter', that those that are designed with economy in mind can stand out.

In conventional publishing, the power of active white space has long been accepted. In the daily newspapers, periodically we see advertisements which take up an entire page, but which might perhaps contain a single entity or small amount of carefully considered text. Yet our eyes which arguably have not been trained to expect this in a newspaper, are drawn to the page, with the result that such advertisements can be very effective in their purpose.

Colour and text considerations

Colours provide contrast and can add character and tonal ambience to a Web page. Likewise, many varying components can make up the total text content in your pages. This chapter tackles these issues and provides some important advice to consider when using colour and text in your Web pages.

Covers

Colours and colour combinations | 48

Working with fonts | 49

Creating effective text content | 51

Allowing for text-only viewing | 52

Chapter Three

Colours and colour combinations

Thinking about the colour of text

Results of recent scientific legibility studies have shown that by and large people prefer to view black text on a white background. White text placed on a black background is often considered the least preferred option as it is generally considered to be the environment in which text is hardest to read – especially on a display monitor.

However, this combination may work better when keeping to larger typeface sizes of the sort used for headings, or text blocks which include only a few words. Perhaps the best advice is to produce your own trial pages and examine closely the issue of text legibility, particularly in relation to text colour and background combinations.

A colour may be considered 'bright', but when overlaid on another colour, the perception may be entirely different. Good contrast between a coloured object and the colour of the space surrounding it, is an essential aspect for clear Web page design.

Perceptions about colour

Different colours can mean different things to different people. Or you could argue that most people don't really care that much about colours used in a Web page, so long as the overall effect is clear and 'pleasing to the eye'. However, colours are used as labels and some colour combinations have special significance in some cultures. So it pays to think a little about the colours you use in a Web page. Consider the following:

- Red and yellow can be considered attention-getting, exciting or warning-type colours

- Green inspires hope and renewal and is a reliable, relaxing, earthy colour closely associated with life

- Strong blue is often linked to the word trust – perhaps this is one reason we often see blue in corporate stationery. In other contexts, blue can also be considered cold, calm or tranquil

- Black can evoke a feeling of space or contrast. White can also help create the illusion of space, and is often linked to cleanliness, sterility, purity or innocence

- Purple or magenta can evoke a rich, regal tone. And so on

Working with fonts

Elsewhere in this book, I've stated that it's important to include a textual description for each graphic used. You could also, consider providing a text-only version of your Web site, or perhaps include equivalent text descriptions of all graphics used, towards the bottom of your Web pages.

A font is a lettering style. You can use different font styles in a Web page, but bear in mind different Web browsers may display the same font differently. Also, ill-considered use of fonts has implications for your readers. One of the most important points to consider is the issue of including a nonstandard font in your Web page. 'Standard' Windows fonts include the Arial, Courier and Times Roman. Use of any fonts other than these does not guarantee they will be available on a visitor's browser.

Standard Windows font Times Roman

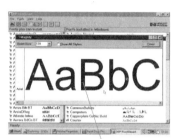

Standard Windows font Arial

Text components take up the least amount of file space compared to graphics, animation and other Web page elements.

Text is generally considered to be easier to read if arranged in narrow column format, like that often applied to newsletters.

If you decide to use a nonstandard font and the required font is not present on a visitor's PC, then the visitor's browser will use the nearest font available that is installed on their PC. So by using a nonstandard font, you may lose control of how your Web page will appear to some visitors. This can have particularly serious consequences if the original font specified has an unusual, ornate or complex spacing structure. At worst, Web page text may be rendered completely disjointed and may even appear as nonsense.

Ensuring a font stays the same: one solution

One way to ensure your readers see what you intend them to see, is to keep to the standard Windows fonts – that is, Arial or Times Roman. Another option to consider which may be useful in some situations, is to convert the line of text containing the desired font into a graphic object. This also has implications: the most obvious of which means the text is no longer text, but must be treated as a graphic object.

HANDY TIP **To find out more about using Adobe Acrobat files, point your Web browser at: http:// www.adobe.com/**

Maintaining a true reproduction of the original

Sometimes, users may want to transcribe a company brochure or a desktop published story onto a Web site. If the choice of font and exact layout is particularly important, one option is to convert your brochure or other important files to the renowned Adobe Acrobat Portable Document Format (.PDF).

PDF files include all the essential information to create an electronic representation of the original document, following the same layout and including any unusual fonts. Also, PDF files are compact, portable and can be viewed on a wide range of different platforms.

REMEMBER **In HTML, you can specify levels of headings, like H1 (largest), H2 (slightly smaller), and so on. Usually, the visitor's browser determines what the text actually looks like. Different browsers may treat the same text differently.**

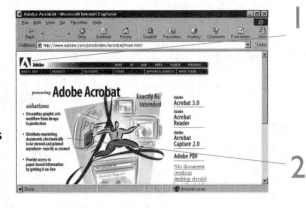

1 Strong branding maintained in a familiar position

2 Quick, clear identification of benefits

HANDY TIP **A horizontal rule is an ideal Web page navigational aid to use when you want to separate blocks of text by subject matter.**

3 A visitor clicks here to download an Adobe Acrobat document

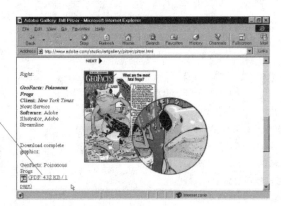

Creating effective text content

Wrapping text around an image can provide an effective combination. The HTML standard includes several attributes which let you do this by using the ALIGN =LEFT, =RIGHT, =TOP, =BOTTOM, and =CENTER attributes. See your HTML guide for more details.

When displaying text, usually, the Web browser decides which typeface and text size to use. You can avoid this limitation by converting the desired text to a graphic. To avoid long download times, only apply this technique to short blocks of text.

Keeping it brief

Remember generally, most people prefer to read long stretches of text from paper rather than from a display monitor. Therefore, consider the following procedure:

1 Make reading on screen easier on the eye for your visitors. For longer stretches of text, you could try to lay out the pages using columns no wider than about 7 or 8 centimetres

2 Keep text content as brief as possible using concrete, familiar words rather than longer or ambiguous words and use shorter paragraphs, especially for complex content

3 Read and re-read each line of text and remove all redundant words and phrases

Or, you could perhaps display an abridged text version onscreen and include a link to the full version so visitors have the option to save the relevant file to their hard drives and print off-line later.

Putting the colour back into text

Many Web pages display their content using black or dark colours on a white background. To help stand out, you can try using a different colour

text. However, the watchword here is contrast: there must be adequate contrast between the background and the overlying text. Furthermore remember, the colour associations mentioned on page 48 can apply in this context too.

Allowing for text-only viewing

On their Web site, Microsoft currently provide a range of popular Web fonts available to download for free. These include: Webdings, Trebuchet, Georgia, Verdana, Comic Sans MS, Arial black and Impact.

On all sorts of pages across the Web, often you can see buttons or icons containing the text:

*   *'Click here ...'* or

*   *' ... to see ..., Click here'*

This kind of text may not actually be text at all but rather a graphic, and not everyone viewing your Web pages will be viewing with a graphics-enabled browser. For example:

*   Some visitors may have the display-related graphics features turned off on their browser, to speed up the Web page display rate on older, often slower machines

*   A visitor may be viewing your Web pages using a text-only keyboard-driven type of browser – I suspect there are still plenty of those in use across the globe

You can prevent these ambiguities by:

To avoid confusion, use the HTML Underline text formatting tag (<UL>) sparingly. Your visitors will probably expect underlined text to be a hypertext link. To add particular emphasis to text, consider using italics or boldface formatting instead.

*   Making sure the text content of your Web pages explains the *essential* points you want to put across

*   Ensuring that each Web page can stand on its own and still make sense to visitors

*   Including the HTML text equivalent of each graphic object used

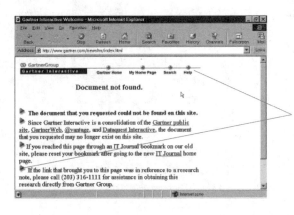

This design shows how even a few carefully placed buttons can help break up a purely text-based presentation effectively

Using graphics

Pictures both static and animated add spice to a Web page, creating more interest and can provide greater impact. However, ill-considered use of graphics can cause more problems for your visitors than they can solve. This chapter examines the issues involved with including graphics in your Web pages and covers the use of different types of graphics and the options available to you.

Chapter Four

Covers

Introducing image types | 54

Considering image size | 57

Establishing colour depth | 58

Interlacing images | 60

Transparent images | 61

Providing impact with imagemaps | 62

Using preview images | 63

Applying a digital watermark | 64

Introducing image types

HANDY TIP

Thoughtful Web site providers often provide large files available in compressed form to reduce the file size and shorten the download time. Once downloaded, visitors can use programs like PKUNZIP/WINZIP to extract the original information, or in the case of self-extracting files, can simply click on the downloaded file.

HANDY TIP

Although pictures help make a Web page more interesting, they can also help break down the language barrier for visitors whose native language is not English. Here the well known saying: *A picture speaks a thousand words* can truly apply.

All sorts of graphics can be included in a Web page. Some of the most striking Web pages use carefully designed images. However, the type of image used in a Web page is important. Here's why.

There are a wide range of image types available: you may have heard of terms like BMP, CGM, PCX, TIF, WMF, GIF, JPG, the more recent development, PNG, and so on, which briefly describe different image types. So for example, the file: SEASCAPE.JPG tells us that the seascape image is a JPG-type image.

For an image to be used in a Web page, it's important that it has been converted to one of the following formats:

•   GIF (Graphics Interchange Format)

•   JPEG (JPG) (Joint Photographic Experts Group format)

•   PNG (Portable Network Graphics format)

These three image formats have been developed especially for onscreen/online use and so are quite compact in terms of space usage. But which type do you use and when: the following pages examine these aspects.

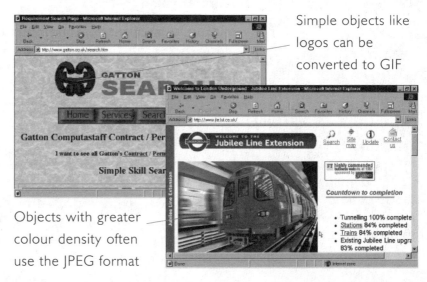

Simple objects like logos can be converted to GIF

Objects with greater colour density often use the JPEG format

You can enrich a Web page by including maps, cartoons, diagrams and photographs as well as visually attractive button icons where appropriate.

 When using a logo on a Web page, convert the logo file to a GIF. However, if a logo is particularly complex, you could try using the JPEG format instead.

 You can include graphics other than GIF and JPEG in your Web pages by utilising 'Plug-in' technology. However, you do need to ensure your visitors have the correct Plug-in installed on their browsers.

What's in a GIF?

GIF or Graphics Interchange Format, was one of the first image formats to be designed especially for online transmission – specifically across the CompuServe network. GIFs are ideal for creating simple Web graphics like logos, icons, buttons and ornate lines.

Logos reinforce branding and if carefully placed can act like signposts or even hyperlinks to other pages or information sources

A GIF image is made up of a rectangular series of dots called pixels. The colour of each pixel makes its own contribution to colours used in the entire image. A GIF image is similar in some ways to the bitmap (BMP) format, commonly used as Windows background wallpaper. However, the GIF format filters out unnecessary information and so is much more compact, reducing file size dramatically.

The maximum number of colours that can be used in a GIF is 256 – an obvious drawback for photographic-type images. Another feature to note is that GIFs can be compressed exceptionally well. Also, if you want to create an animated image, you can link together a series of GIFs to create a dynamic or animated GIF. Providing the illusion of movement to a Web page is covered in Chapter 8, *Animating Web pages*. GIFs can also be interlaced to begin displaying an image sooner. Interlacing is examined on page 60.

A GIF can also be converted to provide a transparent background: this can be useful if you're using a background image in a Web page (see Chapter 5, *The Web page background*).

If the graphics you plan to use are your own, fine. If not, check whether you can use them legally in your Web pages. Copyright is the key word here. The Web is new territory for lawyers and things may not always be what they seem. The safest route is to get agreement to use images in writing before doing so.

If you use an image which is your own, and you want to protect your ownership of that image, include an appropriate copyright notice on every Web page in your Web site. Also, see the section covering digital watermarks later in this chapter.

JPEG - the photographic format

Considering the expanded meaning, it's no surprise the Joint Photographic Experts Group (JPEG) file format is ideal for displaying photographic type images on your Web pages. Consider the following pointers:

- JPEG files are easily recognised as ending with the filename extension .jpg

- Like GIF, JPEG is also a high compression format and can use up to about 16.7 million colours

- However, JPEG files don't convert small text, solid blocks of an image, or hard lines as well as can be achieved using a GIF

The PNG graphics format

A relatively recent addition to the Web graphics format gallery, PNG (Portable Network Graphics) provides a very high compression format, and as such has been hailed as the future graphics format tailor-made for use on the Web. However note: not all browsers yet support PNG. Claims of 30% greater file

JPEG is an ideal format to use when portraying an image containing many different colours and shades

size compression over the GIF format have been made for the PNG. Also note there are different PNG file types for both the PC and the Apple Mac, and PNG images designed for one platform don't usually display at their best on the other platform. One of PNG's most striking and potentially powerful features is that these images can contain embedded textual information (meta-tags) which can be detected by the Internet search engines.

Considering image size

'A picture is worth a thousand words': the time-honoured saying that is often true. However, the use of pictures and other graphics in Web pages has implications of which you should be aware when considering your page design.

One of the most important aspects to consider is the file size of every image or graphic used. By file size, I refer to the number of colours used – or colour depth – as well as the physical size. Colour depth is covered overleaf.

The most important image size indicator for images used in Web pages is the Kb value. Kb is short for Kilobyte, which is equal to 2^{10} (1024) bytes. In Windows Explorer, with the View > Details command active, you can see Kb size of a highlighted image stored on your hard drive.

The physical size of an image is determined by its horizontal and vertical dimensions. Physical size of each image, in addition to other factors, determines the Kilobyte (Kb) size. One benchmark to consider therefore, is to try and make each image used in your Web pages take up less than about 20–30Kb.

Considering download time

The larger the image, the longer it takes to download at the visitor's end. Even a small thumbprint image can use many thousands of Kilobytes if not converted correctly. Your Web page visitors will therefore probably thank you for taking the time to think about this aspect. Also, if your Web pages have different multiple images, then remember the download time increases correspondingly.

When using images in your Web pages, it's a good idea to make sure that you associate a text description with each image used. You can do this easily when you enter the HTML code for your Web pages using the ALT attribute.

Although larger, JPEG-type images help provide an impact, do remember the price to be paid is in download time

Include smaller images or buttons on a Home page and put larger images on supplementary pages

Establishing colour depth

The term colour depth refers simply to how many colours are used in an image. For example, a GIF image may display adequately using 256 colours, whereas another, let's say, photographic-type image may display poorly at this level: perhaps a colour depth of 64K or preferably, 16 million colours would be better here.

While preparing the images you intend to use on a Web page, you could work at high colour depth and larger sizes. Then, when you're ready to place the images, convert copies of the originals down to the desired size and colour depth using a suitable graphics program (e.g. Paint Shop Pro).

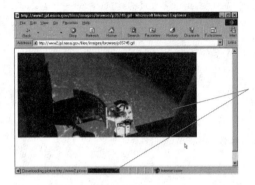

Not all photographic-type images are in JPEG format. This partially displayed image is a non-interlaced GIF. As the page designer, you can decide the best format for your visitors

If possible, aim to keep the colour depth as low as possible for the image you're using: ideally 256 colours for GIFs and 32,768 or 65,536 colours for JPEGs. However remember, image quality should always take top priority.

You may see different images formats being described in terms of bits instead of colours. This is simply another way of describing colour depth. The following table illustrates how colour and bit-depth are related.

If your company logo is not available in electronic format (like GIF or JPEG), you can use a scanner to capture the image from a brochure or letterhead. Then, if necessary, use an image editing program to convert the image file to the correct size and format.

Number of colours:	Is referred to as:
2 colours	1-bit
16 colours	4-bit
256 colours	8-bit
32,768 colours	16-bit
65,536 colours	Also 16-bit
16,777,216 colours	24-bit or 32-bit

...contd

For each graphical component you use, aim to create the smallest graphics file for the best image quality possible.

On computer display monitors, images are best measured in terms of pixels. So when considering image size, think in terms of pixels rather than centimetres. Try to keep photographic-type images to less than 200 pixels horizontally and vertically.

To create tolerable page download times, try to keep the total graphics content of each page to less than about 50Kb.

Keep to the RGB colour model

When designing or converting an image for use on a Web page, note images colours can be made up using different colour models. For example:

- CMYK – **C**yan, **M**agenta, **Y**ellow and **K** (Black) (as used in professional colour printing)

- HLS – **H**ue, **L**ightness and **S**aturation

- RGB – **R**ed, **G**reen, and **B**lue

Remember, computer monitors display colours using the RGB model, therefore this is the format to use when designing or processing all Web page graphics.

Applying colour correction

An image created on a source other than your own computer may not display the image colours properly on your monitor. Essentially, this is due to differences between your computer monitor and the equipment which was originally used to create the image (a scanner for example).

We all see colours differently. When preparing your images, most good graphics applications (like Paint Shop Pro for example) include a command which can allow you to properly calibrate your monitor so that it matches the true colours of an image. Usually, this command is available on the View menu and may be called something like Colour Correction or gamma correction.

Whilst preparing images from other sources to include in your Web pages, if an image is particularly complex, it's a good idea (though not essential) to correct the colour levels using the gamma correction tools in your image preparation software, before converting it to GIF, JPEG, or PNG. In this way, you can see a true representation of the image you're working with and establish better whether it is what you want.

Interlacing images

Downloading GIF images of about 40Kb or more can take a while, and depends on the speed of your Internet connection as well as other factors. However, interlacing offers a way in which larger capacity images can appear to be displayed quicker. Interlacing refers to splitting an image file into two sets of alternate bands. Then, as the image is downloaded on a user's browser, one set of bands is displayed first – at this point, the entire image is visible but is still indistinct. Only when the other set of bands is fully downloaded is the full image clearly visible.

The advantage of using this approach is that visitors can view the essential details of an image before the image is fully downloaded. They can then decide sooner whether it's relevant to what they're seeking, or if not, immediately click on another link without having to wait for the full image to download.

Consequently, interlaced GIFs appear to reduce download times for your visitors – and so represent another important reason to consider using interlaced images often. Sometimes however, a non-interlaced GIF is preferable, for example, when you want to deliberately prevent an interlaced-type of download and provide a sequential display to achieve a desired impact or provide a suspense or surprise element.

Creating an interlaced GIF

You can easily convert a non-interlaced GIF to interlaced format, using any good image editing program. For example: the shareware program Paint Shop Pro, is one such application with this capability.

Progressive JPEG – a similar approach

Ordinary JPEG images cannot be interlaced. However, Progressive JPEG – a more recent development of the JPEG standard – provides a similar feature. When a progressive JPEG image is downloaded, an approximation of the image is displayed on the first cycle. On subsequent cycles more detail is added until finally the entire image detail is displayed.

Transparent images

Sometimes, you may want to place an image on the page, but not want to use the background of the image. For example, you may already have decided to use a specific Web page background, which could be a contrasting colour, a variation of an image, or a pattern in itself. Let's imagine the image you want to place comes with a white background, but your Web page background is of another colour, shade or pattern (as in below left). Such an image could look so much better if the white background were filtered out, allowing your Web page background to replace your original image background (as shown below right).

These two images show how by making a logo transparent, it can become part of the page

There's another way in which you can give the impression that an image is transparent without it actually being transparent. Simply create a darker image on a lighter background and set the page background to the same light shade; for example: white.

Remember, two main image formats are used in Web pages: GIF and JPEG, although the more recent PNG format may become more popular as it becomes more established. Of the two main formats, currently, only GIF images can be made transparent.

How to create a transparent image

The GIF file format comes in two main flavours: GIF 87a and GIF 89a. The GIF 89a standard provides several extra features, one of which is transparent images. To create a transparent GIF, you can modify an existing GIF or create an entirely new one using a suitable application. The *GIF Construction Set 95* from Alchemy Mindworks, is one well known shareware application in which you can create transparent GIFs (also animated or dynamic GIFs, as discussed in Chapter 8, *Animating Web pages*).

Providing impact with imagemaps

Colourful and complex is not always best. Simple line art images, like those found in newspaper cartoons can sometimes be just as effective as more elaborate images.

The Web is essentially a graphical medium. Therefore wherever appropriate, use attractive images on your Web pages. Pictures usually work better than reams of text – and are usually more interesting from a visitor's viewpoint.

Imagemaps can result in larger file sizes than expected. Consequently, this is an area for the Web page designer to watch.

An imagemap is essentially a single, usually larger than 'normal' image which contains two or more links to other Web pages or other addresses on the Web. Specific areas of an imagemap are assigned different link addresses. A visitor simply clicks an area of the image to jump to another Web page or Web address. These defined areas can be irregular in shape or have a more common profile like a button or icon. The illustration on the opposite page shows the opening Web page for the Babylon 5 site which provides an impressive imagemap of what's available.

Imagemaps can provide a neat way of including more links in a smaller area than would otherwise be possible and can be quite effective from a design standpoint. This is one reason why a picture imagemap is often used as an attractive substitute for a menu and series of hyperlinks. However, an imagemap can only be detected by (active) graphical – not text-based Web browsers. As most modern browsers are graphically-based, this fact may not present a problem for most of your visitors.

Including an imagemap in a Web page can be done in two ways: client-side, or more rarely nowadays, server-side. Both methods have benefits and drawbacks. However, with a little more work, you can provide the best option by combining both techniques. See your HTML guide.

Creating an imagemap

An imagemap usually has three components:

- a GIF- or JPEG-type image

- The map data: a text file describing the areas mapped within the image above

- The HTML code that positions the image in a Web page and which specifies it as a 'mapped' image

The easiest way to create an imagemap is to use an application designed for the job. Your browser search facilities can help you find one. Or read the reviews in the computer press and speak to your computer dealer.

Using preview images

Try to avoid including large photographic-type images in your Web pages, *unless* you can justify doing so. A large photograph could take two or more megabytes of space: this can take quite a while to download, especially when using an older 14.4Kbps modem.

When using images from the popular image libraries, check if you can use them on your Web pages. Some image providers may limit the copyright usage. The only sure way you can use an image unconditionally is if you own it.

A preview image is a small thumbnail representation of the 'real' image. As a preview image downloads much quicker than the 'main' image, it's an ideal way to reduce download time while still providing the content. If a visitor wants to see the main image, usually they can simply click the preview image and wait a little longer.

The obvious advantage here is that visitors can choose what to view, rather than longer download times being imposed on them. Use of preview images demonstrates consideration for your visitors and I feel sure will be much appreciated. Another situation in which thumbnail images are useful is when the associated 'main' image is a high resolution, photographic-type image (using the JPEG format).

The important point about thumbnail images is that they introduce choice to your visitors. In fact, my advice is to never provide direct access to any large, photographic-type images: why not provide a thumbnail stand-in and let your visitors decide what action to take and when.

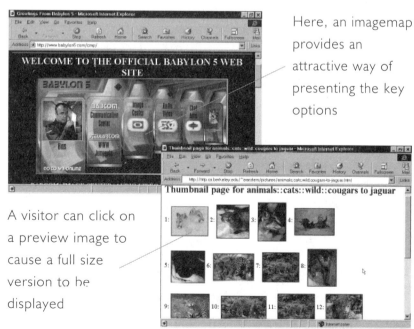

Here, an imagemap provides an attractive way of presenting the key options

A visitor can click on a preview image to cause a full size version to be displayed

Applying a digital watermark

A digital watermark marks an image or graphics file in a special way. This technique can be useful if you own a logo or any other graphic and want to protect it as your own and so apply copyright. Although you can include copyright information on Web pages, this still doesn't stop anyone from simply copying an image. Applying a digital watermark also does not stop anyone from copying your logo or other images, but it can settle a dispute over ownership quickly.

How is it done?

By applying an invisible digital watermark to an image, you can actually embed special copyright information in the file itself in the form of a Creator Identification. This information is not visible, does not interfere with the quality of the displayed image, and can not easily be deleted or overwritten (unless you know how). The copyright information is also available as part of the file, so users can immediately see who owns the image.

Adobe Photoshop is one such application that is capable of embedding a DigiMarc digital watermark into an image. But if you do use this facility, you must pay an annual subscription –
currently around £60 – to DigiMarc for maintaining the image ID database. This could pay for itself many times over if another party contests the ownership of your valuable graphic,

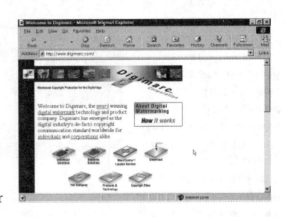

as your case for ownership is almost guaranteed using this type of embedding method.

Use the search engines in your browser to quickly find out more about the different types of digital watermark systems available.

DigiMarc are available at: http:// www.digimarc.com

The Web page background

You could leave your Web page background white or grey and adjust everything else to fit. But why limit your options. Now you can choose from a variety of exciting backgrounds. However, backgrounds can cause some surprising problems. This chapter covers the essential issues.

Covers

Background: exotic or plain? | 66

Using a black background | 68

Creating a picture background | 70

Chapter Five

Background: exotic or plain?

The Web page background can arguably affect the readability of text more than any other design aspect. Contrast is the key word here, or to be more exact, contrast between text and background.

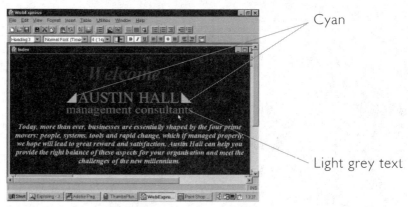

Cyan

Light grey text

HANDY TIP

If you want to use a plain light coloured background but feel pure white is too 'clinical' for your Web page content, try creating a slightly off-white or cream colour to considerably improve the warmth factor.

In this imaginary draft, arguably, the colour combination of this logo against the black background would not contrast adequately

Early browsers would display only a plain grey background as shown below. Newer browsers like Netscape Navigator/ Communicator and Microsoft's Internet Explorer allow both the Web page author and the visitor to 'set' the page background. As a Web page designer, you should decide what type of background is *appropriate*, bearing in mind the general content, image types and other components you want to overlay.

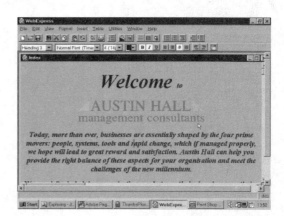

...contd

Embossing a background image

Arguably, one of the most important things to consider when using a coloured background or one which uses an image, is that the overlapping elements like text, hyperlinks and graphics should all contrast clearly with that of the proposed background. If you consider this condition is not met, but still want to use an image for the background, remember there may still be other ways in which you can 'tone down' an image, using a suitable drawing application like Corel PhotoPaint, Adobe Photoshop, or shareware offerings like Paint Shop Pro.

Reading from a computer monitor demands more from the eye than when reading from paper-based documents. When considering the combined use of colours therefore, it's important not to use colour combinations that make reading harder, such as: medium-dark coloured text on a darker background.

One popular option is to make a copy of a proposed background image, then experiment with lighter, embossed effects. This has the added benefits of toning down the image as well as still ensuring that the essentials of the picture are still visible without interfering with the clarity of objects overlaid on the Web page.

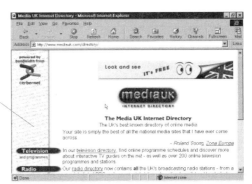

In this example, the designer has chosen to emboss only one section of a framed design with a background image

Using a black background

A black background in a Web page can emphasise expanse like no other effect. A black background can be a powerful design trait to include in your Web page. Black tends to enhance the sense of space and depth. However, the use of such a large expanse of black has implications for Web pages, as the following sections indicate.

In this excellent black background example, BBC2 chose a black background containing a characteristic illumination component, strongly echoing

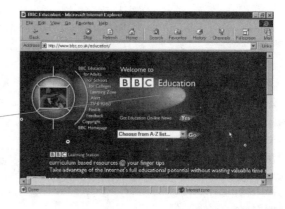

 It may sound obvious but black backgrounds can work well for products that have black associated with them. For example, black has been used in the Guinness Web site to create a stunning backdrop.

the link to television studios. This technique of endorsing the theme of a Web site can work well if considered carefully

Using coloured text with black

Results in recent studies tend to indicate that most people are not comfortable with white (or light coloured) text on a black background. Also, generally people don't like to read a lot of text on a conventional screen. Statistically, reading from a display monitor screen is considered to be 25% less efficient than reading from paper-based pages.

From a Web page design aspect, I suggest anything that interferes with legibility should therefore be treated with caution. This is not to say that any Web page or Web site using a black background is bad or any worse than any other design. In the hands of talented graphic designers or colour specialists, anything is possible – and there are many good examples to be seen on the Web.

...contd

Images: a word of caution

Images placed on a black background can look impressive or dreadful. If the image is good – by that, I mean ideally one that has been designed by a professional graphics artist (or equivalent) – then the results can be stunning.

The essential branding element takes top priority

The well designed PC Pro Magazine Home page includes all the essential components almost in the space of one screen

When using a black background, any small graphic which originally contained a lighter background can be converted to transparent GIF to ensure the page background replaces its original background. Any good graphics application (like Paint Shop Pro) should have the capability to create transparent GIFs.

A scrolling banner provides a moving element containing a brief overview of the site

Clearly labelled colour-coded buttons provide fast access to topics and information

The most important component is placed in the centre

However, if an image has not been designed for a black background, the results may be less than impressive. The point is an image may not be considered 'good' and yet look fine on a white background. Do remember, though, that 'poorly designed' images tend to look worse on a black background, than when laid on a lighter (or white) background.

Creating a picture background

Using a GIF-type picture as Web page background wallpaper can provide an effective Web page design backdrop. However, for this to work, you need to consider several things:

- The HTML standard must be version 3.0 or later; use the BODY BACKGROUND sequence in HTML or equivalent

- To ensure the picture is automatically tiled by the browser, the image should be smaller than the browser window

- It may be a good idea to convert this type of image to a lightly coloured watermark type graphic, to ensure that the background does not interfere with the main message of the page. Also, remember, it's important to maintain adequate contrast between the background and the overlying objects, especially text

A strong picture background probably works best in Web pages which contain limited amounts of text or pages which contain primarily graphical components.

Variations of a background design applied across different types of pages can often work well. In the illustration on this page, Shell have chosen an obvious but effective background link to their company.

Including a background image behind multiple frames

In Chapter 7, *Working with frames*, we examine how each frame can be considered to be a Web page in its own right.

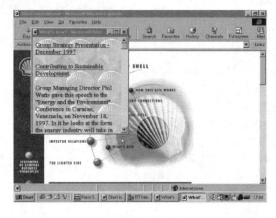

Sometimes, you can achieve an eye-catching backdrop by including an image background which can be made visible between frames. See your HTML guide for more information on applying this technique to your Web pages.

Including tables and lists

Tables can help present content containing a possible mix of text-, numerical- and image-based information more clearly. In this chapter, we examine the aspects of including tables in your Web pages and the important options open to you.

Covers

The value of tables | 72

Some table design options | 74

Using tables in forms | 76

Presenting information using lists | 77

Chapter Six

The value of tables

A HTML table in its simplest form is a grid of cells laid out in rows and columns. Each cell can contain text, numerical data, an image, or even another table. A variety of attributes can be applied to tables. Also, tables and their cells can include different shades, borders or even appear borderless. Therefore, remember a table can be:

Sometimes, you may not even need to use tables to provide the desired effect. When used with careful consideration, simple, unobtrusive horizontal lines can help separate categories and organise text and tabular information to provide a greater sense of order.

- Inserted into the main body of a Web page

- Or placed into a cell of an existing Web page table

In this example, a simple two-column table approach has been chosen. The essential emphasis here is on speed of information access, rather than presentation quality

To create the effect of wider margins within a table, you can increase the level of padding in each table cell.

Commands for inserting and arranging information in table form, represent one of the most powerful aspects of HTML. Although tables are in themselves quite simple, HTML commands provide quite a lot of scope to determine a table's structure and appearance.

Some of the earlier browsers may not display cell background shades correctly.

In HTML, tables behave differently to those found in say a word processed document. In a desktop published or word processed document, tables are obviously designed to fit into a document space and so table sizes can be clearly defined and controlled. With HTML, the target space is the visitor's display monitor – or more precisely – their browser window. The problem is that many different browser and display monitor resolutions are available, so HTML must ensure Web page tables can be resized on-the-fly, when necessary, by the browser.

...contd

HTML tables provide the following benefits for the Web page designer:

Use tables in a Web page in which precision and alignment are important to ensure an enhanced look and feel to the page.

- Enable information to be presented in precise row and column format

- Provide the illusion that text, numbers and images can be positioned independently anywhere on a Web page

- Correct use of HTML tables can ensure neatness and order are demonstrated over a range of browsers

You can create a variety of interesting effects by experimenting with table borders, border widths, cell size, spacing and padding values.

- Web page components can be positioned and aligned precisely without it being obvious a table is being used

Information listed previously applies to those tables created in HTML, either by entering the HTML codes directly or by using a dedicated Web page design application, like *WebExpress* or Microsoft's *FrontPage*. However, you can of course include any table created in a word processor-type application as a graphic if you wish. However remember, in this event, each time you want to change information in the table, you may need to edit the image in the source application and then re-insert it into the Web page.

There may still be browsers available that don't support all the mainstream HTML commands for tables. A visitor using one of these browsers to view tables, may therefore experience unpredictable results.

This example shows how multiple tables can help provide the illusion of a non-uniform design

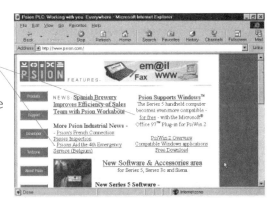

Some table design options

 There are several ways in which you can break the uniform look of a table. Try applying these two tricks: (1) Use spanning techniques to combine cells. (2) Try inserting a table within a cell of another table.

Specifying table parameters

In HTML, the <TABLE> tag can include several attributes which help determine the look of a table, including table width, border parameters and alignment on the browser window. Specifically, table width can be specified as a percentage of the window width, or as a precise value in pixels (however, see the Beware note in the margin).

Table and cell backgrounds

Individual cells, a series of cells, an entire row or column, and even an entire table can have background shades applied. Different shades are often used to highlight cells of special importance. Different shades in cells can also be used with spanning techniques to produce special effects in a table. Usually, the table background takes precedence over the Web page background, however, if no background colour is specified, the properties of the Web page usually apply.

 Specifying a table width precisely in pixels rather than percentages, can provide a high degree of table size accuracy. However, when using precise values, a visitor's browser may be unable to dynamically resize the table to match the viewer's window size.

Applying a variety of borders

Any table or cell can include a border and the thickness of the border can also be specified with your HTML.

Designing a table not to look like a table

A HTML table need not follow the simple row and column grid pattern. If you want to break the rigid grid pattern of a table, you can combine adjacent cells to form a single cell. To help break this rigid pattern, the space occupied by groups of cells can also be combined to form a single cell (spanning). For example, spanning can help :

- Create a neatly aligned table title along the top of a table

- Text appear to flow around both sides of an image

- Create image captions and descriptions

Also, remember a table can be inserted (nested) within a cell of another table. In this way, some amazing effects are possible to present information in a variety of compelling and interesting ways.

Create a Web page newsletter

Another common use of tables in a Web page is to provide a neat two-, three-, or more rarely, four-column newspaper-type display. Here, text, numerical and graphics components can be aligned neatly in narrow columns making the business of reading and scanning much easier on the eye.

 When including a table in a Web page, it's a good idea to test the response of several table sizes by trying out different display windows sizes and screen resolutions, to confirm the information is still displayed clearly.

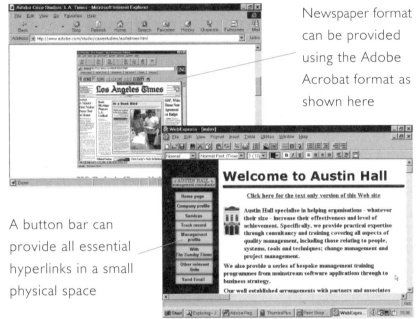

Newspaper format can be provided using the Adobe Acrobat format as shown here

A button bar can provide all essential hyperlinks in a small physical space

 Table rows, columns and cells can have a variety of parameters applied, to create many special effects. See your HTML guide, or get HTML in easy steps, for details.

Create a vertical or horizontal button bar

Several button icons can be inserted in a HTML table to provide a neatly aligned display:

- This can then be placed vertically on the left or right margin

- Or more rarely in the middle of the page

- Alternatively, the same approach can be applied to create a horizontal bar placed at the top, middle or bottom of the page

Using tables in forms

HTML tables used in Web page forms can be invaluable. Here's why.

First, let's assume you're creating a dedicated Web page form. Often, a Web form includes a number of fields into which a visitor may be prompted to enter specific details, like name, address, and so on. If you decide not to use a table in your design, often, each field that's directly below the field above, will not be aligned vertically.

So you can end up with a series of displaced fields which on first viewing looks untidy and 'rushed'. By using tables to lay out the central design structure, all these fields could be arranged in one column, aligned neatly to one edge of the window. In this way, further tables could be used to create other sections of the form also.

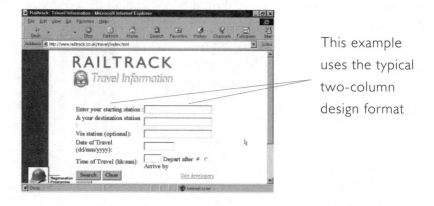

This example uses the typical two-column design format

A common approach is to use a two-column table with as many rows as required. In this way, you can arrange for all the field titles to be placed in the left-hand column and the fields themselves in the right-hand column. Alternatively, you could create a more complex structure which uses more of the width available in the browser window.

Presenting information using lists

Including text-based information in list form provides the Web page designer with another powerful design option. Using the list commands available in HTML, information can be laid out in a neatly defined and aligned format.

Lists can be displayed with bullets, numbered or in plain format. In HTML, a list can also appear multi-levelled and can be nested inside another to provide an indented display of information. Lists help provide:

If you want to display information in a closely defined layout – like a poem for example – sometimes use of the <PRE> tag in HTML provides the simplest solution. Remember, <PRE> preserves the exact character and line spacing/break sequences. <PRE> is also useful for creating perfectly aligned columns of text. See your HTML guide or, HTML in easy steps, for more information.

- A sense of order to a Web page

- A hierarchy of importance of information: indented text under a previous list entry implies a closer relationship to the previous heading compared to other entries

- An indication – at a glance – of a logical structure, flow or sequence

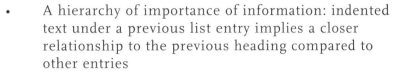

This plain Web site displays information clearly using lists and standard bullets

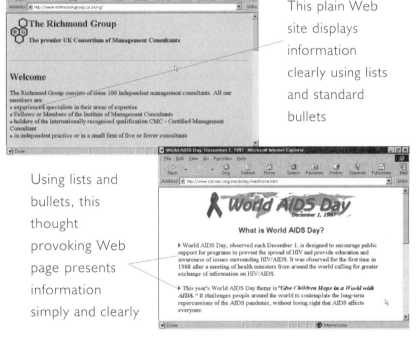

Using lists and bullets, this thought provoking Web page presents information simply and clearly

REMEMBER

In HTML, to create an unordered type list, use the <UL> and </UL> tags. To create an ordered list, use the <OL> and </OL> tags.

REMEMBER

To display a list of terms and their meanings on a Web page, you can use the following Definition-type list HTML tags: <DL>, </DL>, <DT>, and <DD>.

REMEMBER

Although other list commands may be available, some browsers may interpret these commands differently. Usually, only the ordered and unordered list commands behave predictably in most browsers.

Listed information can be displayed in HTML Unordered or Ordered list format. Let's examine the differences.

Unordered lists

In HTML, unordered lists don't have a numbered sequence. Usually, bullets are used to highlight each entry. Unordered-type lists are ideal for displaying:

- Text information which does not have a numbered or logical sequence

- A nonspecific sequence of events

- List entries that can be indented or nested within the previous list item

For example: to display a list of points, just like we've done in the list above in this book.

Ordered lists

The name implies a more structured or sequential purpose. An ordered list:

- Displays the list entries in a numbered sequence to indicate a logical structure, flow or sequence of events

- List entries can also be indented in the same way as unordered list entries. The numbering structure relates each entry logically to its neighbours

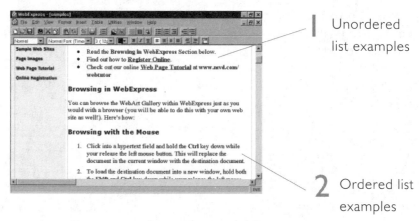

Unordered list examples

2 Ordered list examples

Working with frames

Frames can provide greater functionality, flexibility and an easier-to-use navigation structure to a Web page. However, ill-considered use of frames can cause extra problems for visitors to your Web pages. In this chapter, we tackle the issues involved.

Covers

Why use frames | 80

Introducing frame types | 81

Applying frames to a Web page | 83

Avoiding common pitfalls | 84

Chapter Seven

Why use frames

Frames provide a way in which a Web page can appear to be split into several sections, in which each section can appear to behave independently of the others, almost like having several different Web pages displayed simultaneously. One section could include scroll bars to move around the space in that section. Another could contain content which could be updated either automatically or

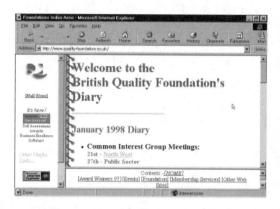

when a visitor clicks on a link in another section (frame) of the page. Clearly, Web page frames help provide wider navigational power for visitors and can also provide more scope for the Web page designer. One of most common uses of frames is to provide a 'fixed' area in which to place perhaps a title or a series of navigation buttons which you want to keep in the same position from page to page.

A series of buttons can be held in place at the left hand side of the screen or towards the top, splitting the Web page into two sections: one scrollable, one fixed. In this way, frames provide the illusion that a Web page is made up of several separate windows.

Why multiple frames can be an advertiser's best friend

In Web pages with an essentially advertising purpose, frames can be particularly useful. Using a framed approach, you can set up your design so that a banner, advertising slogan, or continually updated animation is held in place while a visitor moves in the adjacent frames, scrolling through your Web pages.

Introducing frame types

Frames are now available in a variety of types, however some frame types – for now at least – only work in certain types of browsers like Microsoft Internet Explorer. However, as the Web matures, other browser originators may match the larger vendors like Microsoft and Netscape, and even include their own enhancements.

Types of frames

A variety of frame types can be created in your Web pages. Consider the following:

A Web page containing frames takes longer than its non-framed equivalent to download. If you consider most of your visitors may be using slower Internet connections, you could decide to avoid using frames altogether.

- *Basic frames* – simply set up areas of the screen with standard borders by default. These are usually available in all browsers that support frames. A variety of attributes, colours and shades can also be applied

- *Multiple frames* – several frames are possible. To avoid confusion, I recommend you keep to fewer than three frames, unless you have a convincing reason to include a fourth frame

- *Floating frames* – currently another Microsoft Internet Explorer feature which can provide frames which can be sited anywhere in the browser window

- *Linking frames* – enables a visitor to click on a hyperlink in one frame (say one of a list of buttons) to cause the content of another linked frame to change (the target of the clicked button)

- *Borderless frames* – available with later versions of Netscape Navigator/Communicator and Microsoft's Internet Explorer and can help produce some snappy results

- *Frames containing custom borders* – again, this is a Microsoft Internet Explorer enhancement to-date and which allows you to specify background colours

Images on a display monitor are made up of thousands of varying dots of light. Each dot is called a pixel. Many current display monitors can provide an 800 pixels x 600 pixels resolution, which means 800 pixels wide by 600 pixels high.

In HTML, you can establish frame sizes using number of rows, columns, percentages, or pixels (see margin).

Beware: non-compatible browsers

Although frames offer many exciting possibilities to the Web page designer, do remember that they are a relatively recent introduction to the HTML standard, and as such, perhaps many of your potential visitors may not yet have browsers installed to handle frames. This really relates to how you profile your potential visitors.

Even though browsers like Microsoft Internet Explorer have been available free to anyone who wants them, this does not necessarily mean everyone will take up such offers and update their browsers. Also, many of us have specific likes and dislikes; big names like Netscape Navigator and Netscape Communicator enjoy a loyal following, and sometimes people simply prefer to remain with a familiar browser.

I suspect there are many users who have the Microsoft Internet Explorer version 2.0 browser still installed – and this version does not recognise frames. The same applies to any version of Netscape Navigator before version 2.0. Therefore, if you plan to use frames extensively in your Web pages, do consider the implications.

One possible 'Please-all' solution

One solution to keep most visitors happy is to create several versions of your Web pages, for example you could perhaps include:

- A text-only version, plus:

- A frameless version with limited animation, plus:

- An all singing, all dancing frame-enabled site including the latest Shockwave- and Java-type animations, where appropriate

Furthermore, you could include the variations of HTML frame tags that currently apply in Netscape Navigator/ Communicator and Microsoft's Internet Explorer (as most visitors are arguably using these two types of browser) to ensure maximum functionality for your visitors.

One drawback to using frames, is that to be sensitive to those visitors who can't view frames, you as the Web page designer may feel compelled to produce similar content in at least two formats, essentially doubling your workload.

If you want to provide a kind of grand tour – of say a range of products, a Web site, a building, and so on – a multiple framed approach could represent an ideal design plan.

Applying frames to a Web page

Frames can add more scope to a browser window by splitting the display into what is essentially several separate windows. Each separate window can then include its own set of buttons and scroll bars and other content. However, the use of frames needs careful consideration. Let's weigh some of the benefits against some of the drawbacks:

The benefits:

Frames can sometimes behave unpredictably in some Web browsers. Therefore, whilst designing your framed Web pages, it's a good idea to periodically test the designs ideally using a range of the most common browsers.

- Each frame can be considered to be a separate window and as such, can contain a completely separate HTML document

- A 'fixed' frame is an ideal container into which you can place items that normally would not change from page to page, like a toolbar or standard button links

- Frame links can be tied together so that carrying out an action in one frame can make changes occur in another frame. Some spectacular effects can be achieved using this technique

- A frame can include a border that is displayed or hidden. Multiple frames with hidden borders, with each frame containing its own active content can provide an overall eye-catching display

The drawbacks:

Frames can provide an ideal basis on which to create a highly graphical navigation structure, to include such elements as an array of vertical or horizontal buttons.

- Multiple framed windows usually take longer to download at the browser end; you need to be sure this will be tolerated by your visitors

- Having several frames active introduces more activity; this can confuse visitors or blur the main message of the page

- Some browsers have been known to crash when trying to handle framed information

- Not all browsers can deal with frames. Ideally, you may also have to include an equivalent 'frameless' version for those visitors who require it

Avoiding common pitfalls

HANDY TIP

JavaScript is a recently developed computer language from Netscape Communications. With JavaScript, many of the problems associated with frames have been solved, allowing Web page providers to create more reliable and interesting effects (see the book, *Java-Script in easy steps*).

Although frames can provide more flexibility and 'action' to a Web page, remember not all browsers can deal with frames. Also, results can be unpredictable, which is a condition you definitely don't want, if it can be avoided. As a result of these oddities, frames are often loved or hated, depending on an individual's particular experiences.

However, if you know that most (or even all as in the case of an Intranet) of your target visitors will probably be using browsers that support frames, then you know you can include frames in your designs with confidence. Also note, often the browser Back button may not work properly while operated when viewing a frame-based Web page. Perhaps this is one reason why some visitors may dislike Web pages containing frames.

Avoiding too many frames

It's easy to get carried away with frames; they can provide so much to a Web page. However, to prevent excessive clutter and longer download times, it's probably a good idea to limit the number of frames on a page to ideally two or three, and in rarer situations, certainly no more than four.

HANDY TIP

If you're upgrading an earlier text-based Web site to that of a more graphical nature, you can still use the 'old' HTML pages. On your 'new' Home page, insert a hyperlink to the 'old' Home page. Visitors who prefer to view text-based content can then click on this link if desired, as shown in the illustration.

Including a no frames version

To meet the needs of those users who are using browsers that can't handle frames, you can include equivalent HTML code using the <NOFRAMES> start and end tags.

Information contained between the start and end <NOFRAMES> tags is then used only by browsers which don't support frames, and is simply ignored by any browser that can handle frames properly.

Animating Web pages

Powerful animation and movement-based components can transform an otherwise dull presentation to one that is attractive, compelling and eye-catching. However, more power often means greater consideration and restraint may be needed. In this chapter, we examine what's available and deal with the issues involved.

Covers

Using dynamic GIFs | 86

Applying flashing components | 88

Using Shockwave files | 89

Including Java applets | 91

JavaScript & JScript components | 93

Microsoft's ActiveX | 94

Establishing what to animate | 95

Some advice on what not to animate | 96

Providing for unusual file formats | 97

Some example animated Web pages | 99

Chapter Eight

Using dynamic GIFs

Static Web pages don't include any movement or animation, only text and ideally some graphics content. Dynamic Web pages include components which provide action or movement of some kind. Although the idea of dynamic Web pages may at first seem more appealing, it's possible for this aspect to be overdone.

 Overuse of animation can produce too much movement on a page, creating a condition whereby the visitor's eye is continually attracted to various, sometimes opposing, elements creating confusion. A visitor can then miss the essential message entirely.

Sometimes, a static Web page can be adequate for your needs and it can put over the desired impression simply but effectively. However, if you feel your Web page is missing that 'extra something', one answer might be to 'spice up' the page by adding a dynamic GIF.

What's a dynamic GIF?

From Chapter 4, *Using graphics*, remember, GIF describes a common type of Web graphic. A dynamic GIF is simply several slightly different GIF images linked together to form a chain almost like a film sequence. For example, there may be ten or fifteen frames in such a sequence. Ideally, a dynamic GIF should be carefully designed to produce a small physical size. However remember, a poorly designed and badly prepared dynamic GIF is arguably, worse than using a single still image.

 You can buy dynamic GIFs 'off-the-shelf', or you can create your own using a suitable application like the *GIF Construction Set*, from Alchemy Mindworks. Their Web site is at: http://www. mindworkshop.com

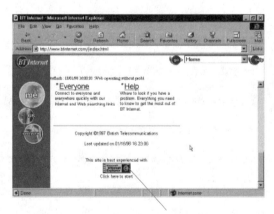

In this Web example, the designers have included the familiar Microsoft Internet Explorer dynamic GIF. Visitors can click on the moving image to be transported to the Microsoft Web site where they can download the latest Internet Explorer software

A dynamic GIF can be set up to:

- Run through its sequence once when a visitor logs on to a Web page

- Loop through a sequence a set number of times. The interval between each frame can also be specified

- Loop indefinitely (see the first Beware warning in the margin)

 Web page elements containing animation demand more from a browser than their static counterparts. Too many dynamic GIFs with infinite loops can use up an excessive amount of a visitor's computer resources, possibly resulting in program and operating system crashes.

 Some users have reported Netscape Navigator v2.0 has sometimes crashed when trying to handle Web pages with frames containing dynamic GIFs. Later versions appear to handle these combinations perfectly.

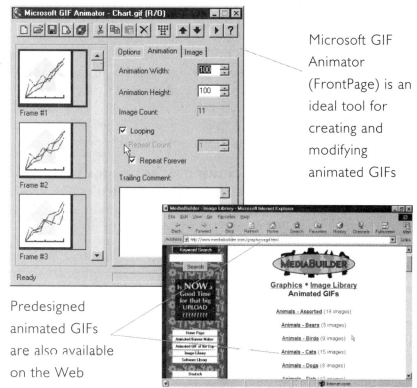

Microsoft GIF Animator (FrontPage) is an ideal tool for creating and modifying animated GIFs

Predesigned animated GIFs are also available on the Web

Dealing with multiple browsers

Some browsers – usually the earlier versions – may display dynamic GIFs incorrectly. Browsers capable of handling dynamic GIFs properly, do so automatically. Those that can't simply display either the static first or last image in the sequence.

Applying flashing components

Paragraphs are usually best left as plain text, as visitors need time to focus on the words and their message. Anything that interferes with this, like flashing attributes, doesn't usually help. Perhaps the one exception to this rule could apply to single headlines or short sentences in which impact or urgency is suggested.

Flashing ticker-tape banners can provide an eye-catching display to communicate something important or to evoke tension.

Information in frames takes longer to download, and so puts a greater strain on slower Internet connections.

Applying a flashing logo to a Web page

If you want to attract a visitor's attention quickly, a flashing logo certainly gets noticed. However, care should be exercised here. By including dynamic elements like this to a Web page, there's a much greater risk of drawing a visitor's attention away from the main message or simply introducing too many conflicting elements. In this event, visitors may miss the essentials of your message entirely.

Also, you may consider a flashing logo will appear too 'loud' or inappropriate for a company or organisation. Some would further argue, such action actually changes the nature of a logo, and as such can cause serious damage to the branding and image of a company or organisation. Therefore, take care and consider the idea carefully before implementing this action in a corporate-type Web page. However, flashing logos in a lighter context do have a place and can work well, when considered carefully as part of the whole presentation.

Including other types of flashing objects

The dangers mentioned in the previous section relating to flashing logos can equally apply to any other flashing object. Consider the main points:

- Anything flashing on a Web page exerts a powerful pull on a visitor's attention

- Including multiple flashing objects on a Web page can create its own special brand of chaos or provide stimulating excitement: the key point here is to carefully establish what is appropriate

A quick way to steal a visitor's attention is to provide a brief line of text and arrange for it to blink. Like a lighthouse beacon, flashing text exerts a powerful pull on the eye. Likewise, a flashing frame tends to draw the eye towards the contents of the flashing frame. If this is what you're aiming for, fine. Also remember, not all browsers can deal with frames properly and remember some earlier versions of well known browsers can't handle frames at all.

Using Shockwave files

Shockwave for Director from Macromedia is a top development product that in the hands of an expert can produce stunning, high quality animated graphics designed specifically for use on the Web. The resulting Shockwave files can only be 'read', however, providing the browser is compatible and has the Shockwave Plug-in installed and set up. Latest versions of Netscape Navigator/Communicator and Microsoft's Internet Explorer are by default, set up to handle Shockwave files.

Web pages containing Shockwave and ActiveX content demand more resources from a PC than those containing more traditional Web page elements. A visitor to a Web page containing these components will benefit fully when using a PC equipped with a CPU of 75MHz or faster.

Shockwave is versatile: text, graphics, animation, video and sound sequences, can all be imported easily. Efficient compression technology ensures these highly animated sequences can be downloaded to a Web page relatively quickly – arguably, this is the most important reason why Shockwave files have become popular on the Web.

'Shocked' components can help bring a Web site alive

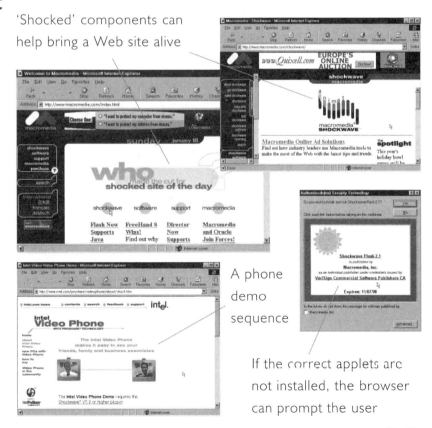

A phone demo sequence

If the correct applets are not installed, the browser can prompt the user

From a Web page design aspect, you can create some compelling and highly attractive elements to include in your pages. However, Shockwave-type animations probably work best when supporting the main theme, made up of more simpler text- and graphic-based components, rather than forming the central elements in your Web pages.

Many of the most visually appealing Web sites include Shockwave files. However, versatility has its price: Shockwave for Director is an expensive and complex program and of course takes time to learn to use.

You can include Shockwave technology (or any other Plug-in) on a Web page using the <EMBED> tag in your HTML document. See your HTML guide for more details.

REMEMBER

A Plug-in is a mini program attached to your browser and which allows your browser to handle unusual file formats.

HANDY TIP

If your Web browser is Shockwave compatible, you can see Shockwave files in action on Macromedia's Web site at: http://www. macromedia.com

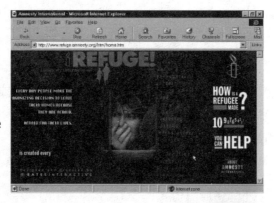

The Amnesty International 'themed' Home page effectively reflects the seriousness of its message

Shockwave in action. Point your browser at the Macromedia Web site (see margin for address)

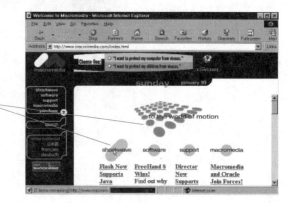

Including Java applets

 It's possible to hide a computer virus inside a Java applet. When a visitor downloads the Web page, the infected applet also runs on the target PC, possibly infecting it with the virus.

Java is a relatively new programming language developed by Sun Microsystems which can enable software developers to create one set code that can be used on any operating system.

A Java applet is a small type of Java program which can be placed independently on a HTML Web page. Examples of Java-type applets include:

- Sophisticated animation sequences, often including sound and video components

- The familiar ticker-tape streamers providing up-to-date relevant news that are often visible on many Web pages, like that shown in BT Internet's Web site below

 If you're planning to include a lot of Java-type applets in your Web pages, do bear in mind, visitors to your Web pages will need to ideally have Pentium-grade computers to benefit fully from the special effects you're providing.

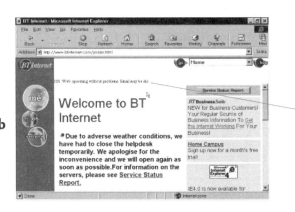

BT's ticker-tape streamer providing the latest news about access to the Web site. Can also be achieved using ActiveX (page 94)

 A Java applet must download to a visitor's computer completely, before it can run automatically.

However, for a Java applet to work, the intended browser must support Java. Two of the first browsers to meet this condition were Netscape Navigator v2.0 and Microsoft Internet Explorer 3.0, and of course, all later versions of these browsers. However remember, although Java offers exciting possibilities, it puts more strain on a PC's resources. Visitors viewing a non-Java Web site would certainly notice the difference in loading speed – especially if they're using slower computers. Consequently, a Web page containing Java components, arguably displays better when viewed using a Pentium-type PC.

...contd

Arguably, three of the fastest ways to turn visitors off a Web site are when it's: (1) boring; (2) confusing; or (3) takes too long to download.

Java is an ideal environment in which to create multimedia files for a Web page easily and quickly. Nevertheless, as with any complex animation technology, usually, from a compatibility standpoint, the preferred option is to include Java files in addition to your standard main components of text and simple graphics. However, do consider, some of your visitors will probably not be equipped to handle Java properly, and this can lead to all sorts of problems – the end result could mean a new visitor leaves your site confused and perhaps even feeling cheated!

To find out more about Java, visit the Sun Web site. Point your browser at: http://www. java.sun.com/

Providing Java applets in your Web pages

If you want to include Java applets in your Web pages, consider the following guidelines:

- You can learn to write your own applets. However, remember Java is a continually changing language with new enhancements appearing almost daily

- Applets which fulfil a wide range of needs have already been developed. Usually, you can simply download these from the Internet and modify them to work correctly in your own Web pages

Java applets can manage data, carry out complex tasks and even do calculations on a Web site.

Java applets are platform-independent: they can run under the Windows, Apple Mac and the UNIX operating systems without the need for modification.

http://java.sun.com/
http://javasoft.com/nav/used/index.htm
http://www.gamelin.com/
http://stat.vol.it/RETE_/javastat.html (to monitor who is visiting a site; plus statistics applets)
http://www.jars.com
http://www.newsbreaker.com (Premier's Web Design Newsbreaker applet)
http://www.riada.com.au/cartel.html (Daniel Adair's news delivery applet)
http://www.sophware.com/ticker/ (good source for financial-oriented applets)

The table on the left lists some excellent Java applet sources.

Remember, to place a Java applet on a Web page, simply use the <APPLET> tag as described in your HTML guide. Use the <APPLET> attributes to fine-tune the placement and alignment of your applet.

JavaScript & JScript components

Think carefully about including Java or JavaScript code which causes scrolling messages to appear in the status bar. These effects generally cause a page to load more slowly, and have been alleged to contribute to operating system crashes at the browser end on some computers.

If you include a feature in a Web page that can only be activated by one system but not the other – JavaScript or JScript – include a text note telling visitors about this precondition.

JavaScript

Developed by Netscape, JavaScript is a type of programming language loosely related to Java, although JavaScript is considered to be less complex and so it is easier to learn. However, like Java, JavaScript has the potential to cause security problems – especially those linked to computer viruses.

JavaScript components can be run as soon as a Web page loads or can be activated by a visitor clicking on a button or other trigger point on a Web page.

Including JavaScript components in a Web page

As with Java, you can learn JavaScript and write your own JavaScript components. Alternatively, you can download predesigned components and modify these to work with your Web pages. Whichever option you choose, it's useful to learn at least the basics of JavaScript (*JavaScript in easy steps* is available from Computer Step: see inside back cover).

You can insert JavaScript using the <SCRIPT> tag in HTML or by arranging for the JavaScript code to run when a specified event occurs. See your HTML guide for options, attributes available and precise instructions.

JScript

JScript represents Microsoft's alternative to JavaScript. Whereas JavaScript was developed with Netscape Navigator in mind, JScript is tightly integrated with the Microsoft Internet Explorer series of Web browsers. Unfortunately, this could mean that some components developed for one technology may not work when confronted with a browser from the alternative technology.

However, with some knowledge of several variations of languages, it's possible to write a script that works correctly in both Internet Explorer and Netscape Navigator, for example.

Microsoft's ActiveX

Lack of Plug-ins can cause problems: visitors using earlier versions of Windows may not have the relevant Plug-in installed. In this event the particular Plug-in technology and special effects will not be available to those visitors.

In some ways, a complement to Java, Microsoft's ActiveX provides yet another exciting Web page embellishment. ActiveX provides multimedia action in the form of animation, virtual reality, video sequences and other types of dynamic content for Web pages.

Shockwave, as discussed on page 89, was one of the first ActiveX controls to be included with Microsoft's Internet Explorer and Windows 95, and so is one of the most well known. Other ActiveX controls include RealAudio as discussed in Chapter 9, *Audio on the Web*.

ActiveX components will run on any computer which has an ActiveX-compliant Web browser installed – like for example, Microsoft's Internet Explorer v3.0 and later versions.

If you plan to use Plug-ins in your Web pages, why not also include a link to each Plug-in host Web site you're using, to provide access to the relevant Plug-ins for those users who haven't already installed them.

ActiveX components are available as shareware. Use the Browser Search facility to locate them

Find out more about ActiveX from information sources free on the Web

To find out more about ActiveX, point your browser at: http://www. microsoft/com/ workshop

Including ActiveX components in your Web pages

To place an ActiveX component in your Web page, you can use the <OBJECT> tag in your HTML document. See your HTML guide for the exact syntax required.

Establishing what to animate

Animated elements can also be used effectively to help visitors navigate through a complex Web site. For example, in an appropriate Web site, you could include a cheerful miniature cartoon character which moves around the screen indicating links to places of interest or to simply direct a visitor where to go next.

Animation techniques can work well when applied to the problem of trying to put over a mass of detailed information. The information can be structured into digestible blocks, and each block only made visible in sequence and by the visitor's movement of the mouse.

As a Web page designer, having the power of Shockwave, Java, JavaScript, JScript, ActiveX, and so on, at your fingertips can provide a great temptation to apply animation techniques to excess. There's no doubt the animation tools mentioned in this chapter are attractive and can provide the main means by which a dull Web site can be transformed into an 'exciting experience'.

However, the key decision is deciding what's appropriate and what's not. Consider the following points:

- The most obvious situation in which animation works is when you want to hold a visitor's attention. For example: to strongly advertise a product or service. However, like most successful advertising, this works best if you can provide another compelling reason for a visitor to stay hooked up. Perhaps use a simple interactive game or quiz to provide the incentive for a visitor to stay and bookmark the site

- If a Web site is dealing with the subject of movement, development or changing states, animation is usually particularly beneficial. For example, when portraying some stages in cooking; or in illustrating the biological growth of an organism; or simply to illustrate the development cycle of a product

- If the subject matter can be interpreted as boring or lacking excitement, sometimes applying creative animation techniques can spruce up a Web page and heighten interest

- Animation does not have to be 'loud' to be effective. Small elements like sparkles or comet-type effects can sometimes make a greater impact

- For subject matters involving concepts that are not concrete or which are difficult to visualise, animation techniques can offer a welcome boost

- Consider carefully the use of animated games and humour on a site which deals with sensitive issues

Some advice on what not to animate

Perhaps in some ways, the title of this section is a little unfair. The truth is there is no easy answer about what not to animate. My guess is that you already know much about the type of visitor you expect to log on to your Web pages. And this knowledge helps define what to include in your Web pages and how to go about it from a design viewpoint. Only you, the Web page designer really knows what is best for your site and for your visitors – although often, this is a learning experience. However, from a general standpoint, consider the following pointers:

If a page includes some animation, it's a good idea to mention this fact so that visitors have an idea of what is going to happen. Also, if you don't, visitors who aren't using animation-enabled browsers may appear puzzled by gaps.

- Don't animate a page simply because you know how to and enjoy creating animations. Usually, it's better to let the purpose of a page dictate its content

- If the central important message of a Web page is text- or graphic-based, including animated elements will probably not help but only confuse the issue

- Visitors essentially seeking information and who become distracted by inappropriate animated elements, may become so irritated that they may leave – getting a visitor to return after having a 'bad' experience, is much harder than trying to win new visitors

- Keep the Home page 'pure'. Animated elements with the additional download time they need, included on a Home page, will probably not be appreciated by visitors who may be unsure that your site contains what they're looking for

1 To provide a 'pure' Web page, carefully select graphics and keep to a minimum

2 Display essential information clearly and concisely

Providing for unusual file formats

Most visitors already have the tools to handle the more usual file types we come across on the Web, like common graphics in GIF and JPEG format, and basic text related files. However, there are many different file types available for download off the Web.

A Plug-in – a small helper application linked to a visitor's browser – can be used to handle an unusual file format which may be included on a Web page. A wide range of Plug-ins and Helper applications are now available. Plug-in technology is available in many browsers including both Netscape Navigator/Communicator and the Microsoft Internet Explorer range.

REMEMBER

For these features to work, a visitor's browser must be able to support the desired feature, either naturally or by having the appropriate Plug-in installed.

For example, let's imagine a Web site provider produces a monthly newsletter. How nice it would be to be able to convert the newsletter to a format that could be made available on the Web site, yet which still keeps the essential design of the newsletter intact. This could easily be done by converting the newsletter to a standard electronic format, like that of Adobe Acrobat (filename extension .pdf).

HANDY TIP

Plug-ins, viewers and Helper applications of various kinds can also be used to handle a wide range of unusual formats, such as ODBC database files and application-specific files like those from Microsoft Word, Excel and PowerPoint.

Adobe Acrobat Portable Document Files can include text, graphics and hyperlinks and once downloaded and saved can be viewed or printed on a visitor's local printer.

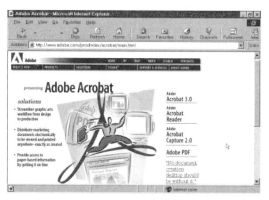

You can view the introductory Adobe Acrobat page at: http://www.adobe.com/prodindex/acrobat/main.html

Dealing with unusual file formats

Firstly, if possible, try to avoid providing information in an unusual format: often, these types of files can be converted to more 'standard' formats. However, if that is not an option, carry out the steps below:

1. Learn about the particular Plug-in you want to use. Often, the best way of doing this is to point your browser at the Home page of the specific Plug-in provider. Here usually, you can glean a lot of useful information and possibly advice

2. Insert the Plug-in content on to your desired Web page using the <EMBED> tag and its attributes in HTML. See your HTML guide for details on the exact syntax to use

3. Mention the name of the unusual format used and optionally provide some brief background information on your Web page

4. To provide the means whereby your visitors can view or use files stored in unusual formats, it's essential to provide a link to the Web site containing the Plug-in application a visitor needs to view these unusual files

5. Ensure the Web link address in Step 4 you provide is valid: test it by downloading the file yourself and running the application

6. Provide brief but clear instructions on what a visitor has to do to view or use the unusual files provided on your Web pages

ActiveX can also be used to make a range of document types available without the need for HTML. See page 94 for more information on ActiveX.

Some example animated Web pages

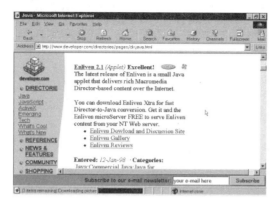

The developer.com Web site is a good source for Java, JavaScript and ActiveX information

While viewing Java-based Web pages, you can view the source code by choosing the appropriate browser command while the page is displayed. In Microsoft Internet Explorer, simply open the View menu and choose the Source command.

Check out the Sun Web site to reveal a valuable information pool about Java

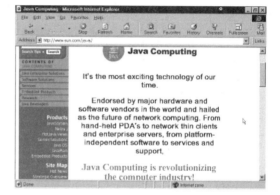

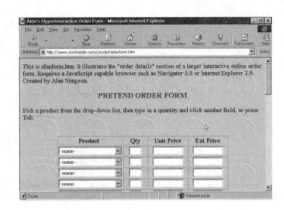

Here's an example online order form designed in Java by Alan Simpson

If you plan to include animated components in your Web pages, the Internet search engines are ideal tools to help you find out as much as possible about the subject you want.

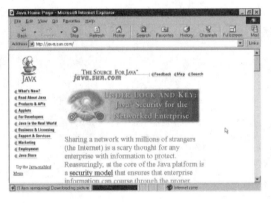

A wide range of information about using Java and other types of animation is available

Some generous parties, like the one shown in this example, provide predesigned animation applets for anyone to use freely

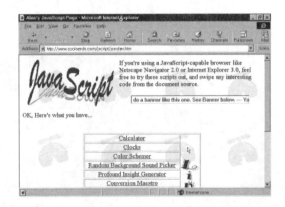

Audio on the Web

As sound is one of the five basic senses, it's natural to think about including sound support in a Web page. In this chapter, we examine the pros and cons of providing sound support in your Web pages.

Chapter Nine

Covers

Introducing the basics | 102

Using simple voice recordings | 104

Including background sounds | 106

Using RealAudio | 107

Providing music | 109

Providing a news service | 110

Audioconferencing: the talking Web | 111

Introducing the basics

After vision, in terms of importance, sound offers the Web page designer many possibilities. Adding sound to a Web page can bring it to life and is especially valuable to those visitors who may be visually impaired.

 For live audio streaming to work, a visitor's browser must be able to support this feature, either naturally or by having the appropriate 'Plug-in' installed.

Pictures may need supporting text to make sense and video clips usually need sound support to be effective. *However remember, sound content can stand on its own without any further support mechanisms needed.* For some businesses – like Web film and music stores – sound is of course an essential ingredient of Web site design.

Visitors however, do need to have a sound card or sound support installed in their computer to benefit. Many PC and Apple Mac owners now have sound support installed and almost all new desktop computers come with sound facilities built in. So let's look at what's possible:

For all sound features mentioned in this chapter, a visitor must have a sound card or equivalent installed in their computer to take advantage of the various sound possibilities, in addition to their browser having the capability to deal with the specific feature they want to use.

- Simple background voice recordings (download entire file first)

- Music sequences (download entire file first)

- Audio sequences played in real time (hear each section of music as it downloads)

- Live audio, talk shows, news, etc. (hear everything as it actually happens)

One important point to note however, is that sound content should not usually simply duplicate what is included elsewhere in text form on your site. You could however, include a brief text description or overview of each audio component. Essential information should always be present in text form, with any audio content 'filling in the gaps'.

Including sound components in a Web page

Sound components can be embedded in a Web page or linked to it. Embedded sound components are usually downloaded automatically when a visitor logs on to a Web page. Linked sound components usually include control buttons to enable visitors to decide if they want to play the sequence.

...contd

REMEMBER

Lots of people read fast; in fact, many can read faster than they can hear. This is one reason why it's important to ensure the essential points of a Web site are displayed in text form. Sound content should always take second place in the importance ratings.

HANDY TIP

Microsoft Windows comes with the Sound Recorder utility. You can use Sound Recorder to record, play and edit any WAVe files you want to include in your Web pages. For more information, see your Windows documentation.

Live audio streaming

Live audio streaming is now available on the Web – or rather, several browsers can now handle this feature. Some Web components have to be download before the content can be sampled: for example, as with many JPEG-type graphic images. With live audio streaming however, live audio content can be played as it's being downloaded to a browser. The big advantage here means a visitor doesn't have to download a large file before being allowed to listen to the content.

Let's imagine, you've designed and set up a Web music store. Wouldn't it be useful for your visitors to have access to a facility which could enable them to download a sample of music, and confirm that it was what they were looking for while the file was downloading.

Benefits and drawbacks of adding sound content

As with any complex technology, there are benefits and drawbacks. Let's consider some of the benefits first:

- Sound stands on its own and adds a new, natural component to a Web page

- The standard sound file formats: those with .wav and .mid filename extensions are ideal providing the sound files of less than about one minute duration

Now let's look at some of the drawbacks of sound content:

- Installing sound elements in your Web pages involves yet another technology, further adding to the technological strains: hardware sound support is required and probably software Plug-ins installed

- Visitors downloading standard sound files (those containing .wav and .mid file extensions) have to wait until the entire file is downloaded to their browser before the sound sample can be heard

- Visitors may become weary of waiting for larger files to download

Using simple voice recordings

The essential power of sound from a visitor's aspect, is that it's simple: they can hear a voice and simply listen while viewing or reading a Web page. Two of the most important benefits simple voice recordings contribute include the ability to provide:

- Background information

- Help or assistance for visitors

HANDY TIP

Entertainers, singers, authors and actors who have set up their own Web pages can also benefit by attaching voice files to their pages.

All without having to cram further visual components on to a Web page. If you're concerned about overloading a visitor's senses – and this is arguably an important consideration – appropriate control buttons can be included in a Web page, passing over total control to your visitors, allowing them to choose when and if they listen by clicking on the appropriate button.

BEWARE

Try to avoid single sentence extracts: don't shorten a voice sequence so much that it has such little value or substance and so irritates visitors.

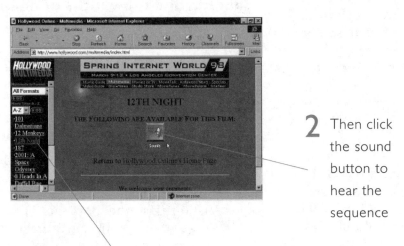

2 Then click the sound button to hear the sequence

In this example, the visitor can first select an option

In the example above, the visitor is presented with multiple options and a lot of control. The horizontal toolbar also includes the 'MovieTalk' button hyperlink to provide further access to a range of interesting voice files.

...contd

'Humanizing' the Web

One of the most powerful aspects of voice recordings is that the human element is immediately evident. Although the Web is a powerful medium, even with all the 'bells and whistles' available, it has still an essentially electronic, distant 'feel' to it.

Contrastingly, the tonal highs and lows of a voice recording, can put over personality and individuality, to include essential human traits. For example, familiar voices from our favourite celebrities can also easily conjure up visible images teasing our memories to enhance the effect further.

However note, visitors can become irritated if a voice recording continues longer than they expect. Therefore:

- Always try to aim for the minimum time possible

- Have a specific purpose in mind

- Try to avoid cramming too much into the sound sequence

- And try to include a brief note stating the expected duration of the recording

HANDY TIP

Some of the latest presentation software packages include Plug-ins which can enable a Web page provider to broadcast a presentation on the Web. To gain further information, check out the latest versions of Lotus Freelance Graphics and Microsoft PowerPoint.

| In this RealAudio example, there's a value here showing just over 6 seconds of the file has been played

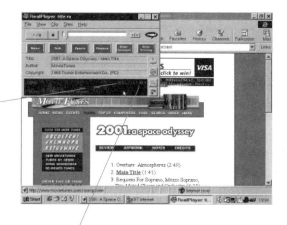

2 Here the visitor can see there is 1 minute 43 seconds in total

Including background sounds

The <BGSOUND> tag works only in those browsers which support it (like Microsoft's Internet Explorer).

Some visitors may become irritated by your choice of background sounds. Therefore, it's always a good idea to provide a mechanism or button to mute the sound content in your Web pages.

Most modern browsers can cope with sound files. However, sometimes different HTML commands are required at the designer end to allow processing.

Background sounds can make an ideal accompaniment to a Web page. Sounds can be converted into several popular formats for use in a Web page, including for example:

- WAVe format – the common Windows format, with the .wav filename extension

- MIDI – Musical Instrument Digital Interface: another popular format often used to tie in with musical instruments and synthesizers. Files can be identified with the .mid filename extension

- AIFF – designed for the Apple Mac computer series and comes with the .aiff filename extension

- MPEG – the Motion Pictures Expert Group, also used for video files. Contains the .mpg filename extension

- RealAudio – as discussed opposite contains the filename extensions of .ra or .ram

Often a simple piece of music in WAVe (.wav) format can be easily set up to provide an audio backdrop and help create a desired mood. Both music and voice accompaniments can also be played either when:

- A page is displayed

- A visitor clicks on a specific button or moves the mouse over a designated location on the screen

Preparing sound files for a Web page

WAVe files can be created easily using the Windows Sound Recorder utility, usually accessible by clicking the Start button in the Task bar, followed by Programs, Accessories, and finally the Multimedia command. You can also create files in other formats using one of the many dedicated sound recorder applications available.

For visitors using the Microsoft Internet Explorer browsers, sound files can be set up using the <BGSOUND> HTML tag to play a specific number of times, or continuously whilst the page containing the sounds remains displayed.

Using RealAudio

RealAudio is a relatively new Web page sound delivery technology from Progressive Networks, which allows sound to be heard as soon as its associated file starts loading in the visitor's browser. Unlike .wav and .mov files, visitors don't have to wait until the entire sound file has been downloaded before listening to its content. With RealAudio, providing the Web page connection is maintained, visitors can browse through RealAudio content, choose a file, and then simply play it if desired. Web pages can include content to enable visitors to listen to RealAudio concerts, live music and talk shows.

 You can find out more information about RealAudio technology from Progressive Networks Web site at: http://www. realaudio.com

RealAudio started with three levels of support: RA1, RA2 and RA3. RA1 provides basic sound quality and was designed for slower 14.4Kb modems. RA2 was much better and provided FM-type sound quality and required a modem speed of 28.8Kb or faster. RA3 also delivered FM-type quality sound and was designed for modem speeds of 28.8Kb and above, plus the much faster ISDN telephone lines. RA3 also includes support for stereo sound channels and various styles of music like, pop, classical, and instrumental. RealAudio version 3.0 also includes the following several components:

 To hear RealAudio content, a Web page visitor must have a compatible browser as well as compatible hardware sound support installed and set up in their computer. Some motherboards have sound facilities built in. Most however, require a suitable plug-in sound card.

- RealAudio Player – to enable a visitor to hear RealAudio files through their browser

- Player Plus – offers a higher quality, CD-type music standard, plus an ability to scan the Web for appropriate files

- RealAudio Encoder – to convert and compress standard audio files into the RealAudio format

- RealAudio Server – allows you to put RealAudio files across the Internet

However, closely following RA3, RAs 4 and 5 emerged, building on the RA3 standard. Different Internet Service Providers may also offer different levels of RealAudio support for commercial and personal account customers. So check what level of RealAudio support they offer.

Creating and preparing RealAudio files

Standard sound files like those with the .wav and .mid filename extensions recorded in Windows need to be converted to the special RealAudio format before they can be used in a Web page. Remember:

- A RealAudio Encoder is required to convert and compress standard files into the RealAudio format

- The RealAudio server allows you to set up and transfer RealAudio files across the Internet and the Web

To sample RealAudio, try the Sony Web site at: http://www.sony.com/music/multimedia/realaudio30.html

These components are usually available for download from the Progressive Networks Web site (address shown on page 107). Also, Wizard-driven applications are now available to make the job of installing RealAudio content on to a Web page much easier.

What a visitor needs to hear RealAudio

To hear your RealAudio files, a visitor's computer system must meet three conditions:

Radio stations too can now deliver their content to surfers on the Web using RealAudio technology.

- Support for RealAudio at their Internet Service Provider. Most good ISPs already support RealAudio technology (but do check the level of support)

- Hardware sound support in the computer: usually, this means a sound card correctly installed and set up

- The RealAudio Plug-in correctly installed and set up for their browser

Play / Pause and Stop buttons

Sound file details

Update window

Progress indicator

Web access

Volume control

Mute button

The RealAudio Player

Providing music

Music can affect people in a variety of ways. If you want to put over a particular mood in a Web site, musical content can help considerably. Consider the basics:

- Fast, dynamic music emphasizes action, tension or excitement

- Contrasting of course, slow and lingering music can help evoke a feeling of calmness and relaxation

- Also, the right kind of music for a Web site doesn't need any further explanation: it is its own language

As a Web page designer, there's a rich variety of musical options open to you. However, do remember longer sequences can put a greater strain on visitors' computer resources. Whilst shorter bursts are less open to error and can sometimes be just as effective.

 REMEMBER

If you're trying to create a particular mood, arguably, the musical content of a Web page usually works best if it contains characteristics that make it soothing and calming, rather than exciting or stirring.

Although obvious openings for musical content include: music/video Internet vendors and games vendors, anyone can enhance their Web pages with some carefully considered musical excerpts, for example:

- An English gardening site could include a few bars of an English dawn chorus carefully recorded at daybreak in Spring

- A geographical Web site with an Australian interest could include a few bars featuring the traditional Aboriginal didgeridoo to invoke the mood of the outback

- A corporate site could include a confident, powerful and stimulating few bars – just as the Home page is loading and the corporate logo emerges

- Let's imagine a travel-based Web site is running a holiday promotion to say, Mexico. A few bars of traditional Mexican music can really set the scene as photos of Mexican culture and scenery are teased on the computer monitor with latest travel offers temptingly woven into the presentation. And so on!

Providing a news service

To provide a Real-Audio-based news service, simply follow the guidelines listed in the RealAudio section earlier in this chapter.

It seems almost anything is possible on the Web. Audio news services are now broadcasting on the Web using RealAudio technology (usually). Currently, only the larger organisations have the resources and money to lay on this type of service. However, the Web has a history of rapid change so if you're interested, watch this area. Some news organisations even provide a text-based equivalent of their audio content for those visitors who want to keep their news viewing more private.

Providing a news service on the Web stretches the resources of the Web and does bring with it problems, the most important of which is really all about maintenance and upkeep. The big problem is that news happens all the time and of course events can change fast, and this can create huge logistical problems for its Web site providers.

There's nothing to stop individuals providing RealAudio background introductions to their Home pages also. For example, sound content attached to CVs can separate you from the crowd.

Fine-tuning a news service

Even considering the previous paragraphs, there's nothing to stop Web site managers however, creating a carefully crafted news service that's relevant to visitors of their Web pages. For example:

- Companies and organisations can include speeches and interviews made by key industry movers and shakers

- Travel-oriented Web sites could include up-to-date news about travel conditions in key parts of the world

- Web sites covering sports events like the round the world yacht races, could include up-to-date news reports about the latest developments

Sound files, like any other format, can have copyright applied to them. Make sure you have appropriate permission to include these where necessary.

- Fashion-based Web pages could include talks from famous designers and models about the latest trends to hit their industry. And so on

However, for these to work properly, the content has to be worthwhile enough for visitors to want to log on again and again to the site.

Audioconferencing: the talking Web

So far, we've examined many tools and techniques which can be applied to spice up your Web pages. However, the Web is a dynamic, fast changing and arguably still untapped environment with many new avenues unexplored.

One thing we haven't mentioned until now is actually talking live on a Web site – or to be more precise audioconferencing. In fact, audioconferencing is a sort of upgraded and more formalised version of online chat in which people communicate across the Internet by typing messages using their keyboards.

 Provided you have Windows 95/98 installed; a 14.4Kbps or faster modem; a sound card (or mother-board sound support); speakers and a microphone installed in a PC, you can try out audioconferencing. Download the audioconferencing client OnLive! from the OnLive! Web site at: http:// www.onlive.com

Audioconferencing can also be considered to be a cross between telephone conferencing and videoconferencing in which several people can take part. Let's learn more about audioconferencing and first look at the main benefits:

- A comparable amount of information to that of full videoconferencing can be exchanged, but without the added complexities and technical demands of all that videoconferencing requires

- Avatars – graphic representations of each member – can be used to provide individual graphical feedback

- Several users could share a single microphone and PC making further savings. Single- and multi-contributor conversations are also possible

- Using stereo speakers, voices can be localised left or right to help create a more natural discussion environment

- A replying voice can appear closer or further away depending on the position of the avatar in relation to the other contributors

- Cost savings in telephone charges can be made – especially significant when used internationally

- Can provide an ideal platform for buyer/seller-oriented Web sites as well as those relating to music, sport and theatre

- Audioconferencing can also provide an ideal environment in which to informally discuss a range of issues, following in the Internet café and virtual clubs tradition

- Finally, audioconferencing could provide an ideal base on which to formulate a unique customer service/support facility or perhaps a training wing

Now let's look at some of the drawbacks:

- Internet traffic can become heavy affecting services, so this technology may not be ideal for mission-critical conferences (However, results over a private corporate Intranet should fare much better)

- There's a lack of genuine visual images of the participants. Instead Avatars, or approximations are used

- Because a true picture of recipients is currently not available in this type of system, the full range of mannerisms is not provided. This could lead to ambiguity and confusion

- Every community has its share of people who enjoy causing trouble. An open audioconferencing facility could open the doors to these kinds of problems

Examining the lists above, clearly there appear to be more benefits than drawbacks, however, there may be other potential Web-related problems present which I've not yet touched upon. Also, this is an emerging technology and as such may still have much to show.

Nevertheless, as the technology is here now, perhaps many Web sites may include audioconferencing facilities sooner than we think. Perhaps you could include audioconferencing in your Web pages and immediately put yourself in a separate league from the main throng.

Audioconferencing when installed in an 'open' Web site, may need careful consideration and management to avoid problems with isolated individuals who might want to discredit the site, hurl abuse, or simply cause havoc for its own sake.

To find out more about audioconferencing, try pointing your browser at: http:// www.thesite.com/ talk/talkmain.html

Working with video components

There's nothing like a moving image to steal our attention – especially when the subject matter is a living, breathing entity. Video sequences can provide the 'icing on the cake' for a Web page designer, but the technology is demanding. In this chapter, we examine the benefits and drawbacks, and include some hot hints and tips to help make your Web video experience a successful one.

Chapter Ten

Covers

Introducing Web video technology | 114

Using RealVideo | 116

Web video hints and tips | 118

Introducing Web video technology

Video technology allows films, TV excerpts and news coverage to be made available through a Web page. However, Web page video sequences can, perhaps understandably, put heavy demands on end-user computer technology. Nevertheless, consider some of the benefits:

For live video streaming to work, a visitor's browser must be able to support this feature, either naturally or by having the appropriate Plug-in installed.

- Video is humanising: it can put over warmth, personality, emotion, feelings, tension and passion like no other Web component

- It's an ideal vehicle for delivering film and television excerpts

- Some international visitors to a Web page may understand spoken language better than written language

If the subject matter in your Web site can be considered boring, often video sequences can heighten interest and help bring a Web page to life.

- A picture is usually better than a thousand words when trying to put over complexities – and if the picture is moving, that's even better

- Video is an ideal advertising medium

Now some of the drawbacks:

- The technology is new, still developing and is complex. Many would also argue that video sequences are not necessary – certainly they should not form the central components of a Web site, but rather supplement or support the main theme

If you embed video files into a Web page, these files can be large and so can affect the download time of a Web page dramatically.

- Just because video is 'available' and fashionable, it doesn't necessarily follow that it's the right choice to use. Spoken language may be difficult to understand. A bad video can actually damage the credibility of a Web page. Therefore, video strategy should be considered carefully to avoid creating more problems than it solves

- Ill-considered use of video can increase the danger of overshadowing the central message – which should always be text-based

...contd

Current common formats

Many Web page providers include the following video file formats available for download:

- AVI files – the standard Video for Windows format (filename extension .avi)

- Apple's QuickTime (filename extension .mov and .qt; usually requires installation of a Plug-in to play these files)

- MPEG – the Motion Pictures Expert Group format

- RealVideo – the latest 'on-the-fly' format (see over)

If the video sequence you want to use is brief, Macromedia Director files like the highly compressed Shockwave files are smaller and therefore usually download quicker than conventional video files.

The main 'traditional' sound and video formats (illustration shown in reverse video for clarity). The latest format – video streaming – is described overleaf

If movement is an important feature of your Web site, a video sequence can arguably illustrate what you want to put over better than any other type of content.

Including video components in a Web page

Video components can be embedded in a Web page or linked to it. Embedded video components are usually downloaded automatically when a visitor logs on to a Web page. Linked sound components usually include control buttons to enable visitors to decide if they want to play the sequence.

You can provide a video component to a Web page using the <A HREF="...">...</A> sequence in HTML, just as you would link with any other file. See your HTML guide for more details. If you're using a dedicated Web page development software, the task is usually much easier: see the accompanying documentation for precise instructions.

Using RealVideo

Early Web video technologies meant a video file had to be downloaded before it would play. However, live video streaming is now available. This means a visitor can play and view a video clip while it's downloading. In this way, a visitor does not have to download a large file before perhaps realising that it was not what they really wanted.

One technology that is making this significant breakthrough is RealVideo from Progressive Networks. RealVideo works in a similar way to RealAudio and provides live video streaming that enables video to be downloaded to a Web browser reasonably quickly. However, video makes more demands, takes longer to download, and so requires a greater accuracy and processing contribution. RealVideo offers other significant advantages over previous Web audio delivery systems, consider:

 A fast ISDN Internet connection provides an ideal environment in which to view RealVideo files. Although ISDN is still comparatively expensive, prices are expected to fall substantially in the next few years.

- RealVideo players installed on visitors' PCs can sense when there's heavy Internet traffic and compensate to minimise problems which may develop as a result. RealVideo aims to provide the most stable picture quality possible under varying conditions

- Additional controls like fast forward, rewind and search are easier to integrate with RealVideo streaming technology

- RealVideo also includes better error correction

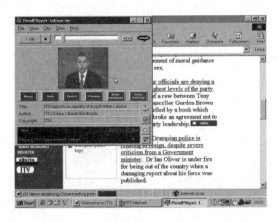

Here, RealVideo technology is used to provide a video sequence from the UK ITN Online Web site using the Microsoft Netshow browser software

...contd

Including RealVideo components in a Web page

To include a RealVideo component in a Web page, carry out the following steps:

1. You can provide a RealVideo sequence to a Web page using the A HREF= link sequence in HTML. The only difference is that the converted RealVideo file should have the correct filename extension (for example: .rm standing for Real Media). See your HTML guide for precise details

If you intend to use RealVideo files in your Web pages, why not provide a link to the RealVideo Web site, so those visitors who have not yet installed the player, can download and install the software.

2. (Optional) If you're using dedicated Web page development software, the task is usually much easier: again, see your accompanying documentation for precise instructions

3. (Optional) Include any other HTML attributes to establish the position at which the video sequence plays on a visitor's screen. Also, you can usually set the number of times the video sequence plays and the size of the playing window

4. Whatever method you choose, test your work. Once a visitor clicks on the link on your Web page representing the RealVideo file, the RealVideo player installed on their PC starts up and plays the sequence. Buttons are available offering fast forward, rewind and search

Live video and audio streaming can now provide up-to-the-minute news. Archived video files can be played back on demand

Web video hints and tips

Although workable video technology appears to be available at last, you still need to consider whether video is 'right' for your Web pages. Consider the following pointers:

- Arguably, few visitors will wait more than three or four minutes waiting for a file to download. If you decide to use Video content, try to keep files sizes small to minimise waiting time

- Remember, some Web surfers may still be using slower 14.4Kb modems. Downloading video files at this speed can take so long as to make a high video content-based Web site almost impractical

- If you want to put over a mood of fast action, changing scenes or subtle movement, video can provide one answer. But, if you want to encourage pause and consideration, usually, it's best to stick with carefully crafted text and graphics content

Information in the form of a presentation can now be broadcast from a Web page, and can include sound, video, and animation components. Lotus Freelance Graphics and Microsoft PowerPoint are two such packages that include the Players to do this.

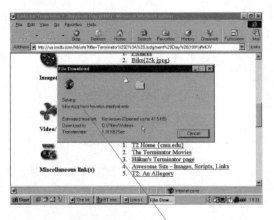

When downloading large files, often the File Download box appears. Remember, visitors will not usually endure download times of longer than a few minutes, at most, unless they've a valuable reason to complete the task

Creating 3D Web pages

We live in a 3D world, so why not enrich a visitor's experience by creating Web pages that reflect the real world we live in? This is what the Virtual Reality Modelling Language (VRML) seeks to do. In this chapter, we examine the use of 3D and VRML techniques and what they can offer to a Web page designer.

Covers

Why use 3D on the Web? | 120

Virtual Reality Modelling Language | 121

Using VRML in business | 122

Chapter Eleven

Why use 3D on the Web?

We see and touch and think in 3D, so it's natural to try and extend this to a Web page. Most of the time, Web sites are displayed in two dimensions – often using a brochure – or newsletter-type delivery approach. Arranging to view in 3D reintroduces depth and brings us back to what is arguably more natural surroundings. This has benefits for Web page designers: having the capability to view an object and then turn that object around to examine what it looks like from all angles, provides a much better picture of what an object comprises of. For some complex objects, the ability to move in 3D could be considered essential – medical uses for example. The all-encompassing term 'object', used in the previous sentences, could of course be modified in other ways for use on a Web page. Consider:

REMEMBER

For visitors to benefit fully from 3D – particularly VRML – usually a relatively fast PC is desired. I suggest at least a 133MHz Pentium-type PC with at least 32Mb of RAM. A 486-based computer would probably struggle and therefore frustrate visitors.

- Taking an imaginary tour around a new type of car engine in a motor company Web site

- Examining skeletal structures from all angles in a medical-oriented Web site

- Browsing through the aisles of a virtual store. Pick up goods and examine them before purchasing

- Watching a living entity grow and mutate in a natural history oriented Web site

- Finding your way around a large University complex using a 3D map

- Moving through the fascinating corridors of a top museum or picture gallery. And so on

Virtual Reality Modelling Language

VRML isn't the only technology providing 3D on the Web. Another, approach, panoramic video, uses 360 degree video. Here, full photographs are taken of a scene. A viewer can then view through a window of about 30 degrees. A user can use the mouse or keyboard to change the view in the current window to include any part of the photograph.

Currently, no one owns the VRML standard although many are contributing to its development. To view one well known VRML source, point your browser at: http://www.viewpoint.com

The Virtual Reality Modelling Language (VRML) is yet another computer language and an emerging standard undergoing regular updates and revisions and which essentially tries to simulate the way we interact with the world.

VRML attempts to provide an imaginary space in which multiple individual components can be displayed naturally, and made to interact with and move around each other. VRML components can now be included in Web pages. Although this technology is still in its infancy, VRML is developing fast. The current VRML version, 2.0 – affectionately called the Moving Worlds standard – includes contributions from a wide range of top software authorities and offers some exciting possibilities, including:

- The ability to handle a wider range of 3D environments

- Aims to provide an open platform-independent base to encourage contributions from different technologies (Windows, Apple Mac, and so on)

- Can include animated components

- Includes more scope for providing realistic real-world behaviour

Including VRML in your Web pages

VRML is not currently part of HTML. To create a VRML environment, you need to use special development tools. These are available for several different platforms. Examples include: 3D Internet Designer from Data Becker; Virtual Home Space Builder and Internet 3D Space Builder both from Paragraph International.

Any piece of complex new software takes time to learn, however, to ensure your Web pages stand out from the mass competing for visitors' attention, the results could be well worth the effort required.

Using VRML in business

VRML offers special benefits to businesses that are only recently being fully realised. Access can be provided to documents, databases and many other information sources all in 3D space. Applying VRML techniques can include the following areas of a Web site:

HANDY TIP

Internet Explorer users can install Microsoft's VRML v2.0 Plug in, available from the Microsoft Web site. Then when you log on to a site containing 3D content, the Plug-in starts automatically.

- Those with high *entertainment* value – computer games in particular have been using 3D techniques successfully for some time

- VRML can help make *navigation* through a Web site easier

- Complex themes can be *visualised* better

- Effective *simulations* can be performed, possibly saving time, money and even lives

- VRML 3D provides a *closer approximation* of what 3D is attempting to simulate

For businesses and organisations, 3D has a natural home in the areas of:

REMEMBER

To participate in VRML, a visitor's browser needs to be VRML compatible. This means either having the appropriate VRML Plug-in correctly installed, or using a dedicated VRML browser.

- *Retail shopping* – here we can imagine the virtual supermarket concept and apply this to any business, large or small

- Some areas of *Research* – complex mathematical and graphical data in particular can be presented better

- Many areas in the world of *work* – some not yet defined or even realised

- Computer-type interactive *games* – in fact, arguably, this area has been and still is the driving force behind 3D development. However, often these techniques can be applied to other areas successfully and indeed the business world is quickly realising the benefits VRML and 3D can bring

Designing the Home page

The Home (or Index) page is what a Web page visitor sees first. Its design therefore, is crucial in helping achieve a desired response. In this chapter, we examine different types of Home page and examine some of the strategies that can help make a Home page successful.

Chapter Twelve

Covers

A generic Home page | 124

A personal Home page | 126

A Home page for doing business | 128

Encouraging visitors to return | 133

Avoiding dead URL links | 135

The email link | 136

Creating an electronic signature | 137

A generic Home page

Generally, people don't like to read text on a screen – if given the choice. So it's a good idea to keep text paragraphs brief, clear and to the point.

After designing and publishing your Web pages, it's a good idea not to later move established URLs. There's a higher risk that these may not be updated properly resulting in a dead URL error message for visitors. Plan ahead and plan carefully to avoid these problems.

It's a good idea to prominently place on the Home page, a note stating which browser(s) work best when viewing your Web pages.

The Home page is a little like the front door of your house: it's one of the main components your visitors see when they log on to your Web site. For businesses, a Home page can also be likened to the front cover of a brochure; sales literature, a newsletter or a magazine.

The term 'page', in this context, is used loosely as a Home page can include much more information than a single screen can hold. In this event, visitors can then use the scroll bars to move down to the desired part of the page.

Deciding what to include in a Home page can sometimes be tricky. Once we realise how important the Home page is, there's a great tendency to include far more than perhaps we should. In fact, often we can create a better Home page by establishing what to leave out *after* deciding what we think we need to include.

To avoid overloading visitors with too much clutter at 'Your front door', it's a good idea to limit the number of distinct information chunks to no more than ten on the Home page – fewer if possible. Meeting this condition should also help to create the feeling of space and put over a sense of planned expectation.

A 'personal' Web page performs a different purpose to that of club or business-related Web sites, and should therefore include only relevant components appropriate to their design. These aspects are examined in more detail later.

Making an impact with simple things

On the Web, just as in other areas of life, first impressions count. Although most people are reasonably forgiving, to leave your visitors with a favourable impression, it's essential that your Home page *and* every other page in your site meet three simple conditions. Every page should be easy to:

* Use

* Navigate, and

* Understand

...contd

To help minimise effort required **by your visitors, try to fit all text and graphic elements for the current page into one screen. Less scrolling can then help ease eyestrain.**

The power of a toolbar

Examples of good Web sites display a thoughtful layout and include navigation aids on *every* page – not just on the Home page. A popular way of providing this feature is to use a toolbar offering a clear at-a-glance outline of the entire Web site structure.

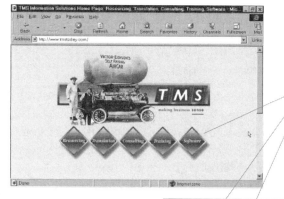

Each of these Web pages demonstrates effective toolbar design.

However, each uses a different approach

When designing or including **button icons in your Web pages, remember by definition buttons are small graphics, so don't try to include too much detail here. Make the purpose of a button instantly recognisable.**

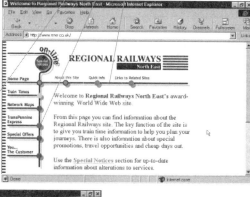

The Home page represents an ideal **point at which to fire peoples' imagination and engage their brains, provide drama or make an impact!**

A personal Home page

Anyone who wants to set up an effective personal Home page is on a mission. For corporate Web page providers, the benefits of setting up a Web site can be more readily defined. For individuals however, the reasons for getting on the Web should be even more clearly defined.

Many individuals provide a Web page without having any real reason for doing so other than to perhaps enjoy the spectacle of seeing their name in cyberspace. Of course, there's nothing wrong with that approach – the Internet and the Web are all about freedom (or chaos, depending on your viewpoint).

Don't forget design options like 'client pull' which can be used to display a 'temporary' Web page which then automatically downloads a following page. This approach could provide an ideal Welcome page which then disappears to display the main opening page. See your HTML guide for details.

It's not difficult for anyone to establish a Web page. However, providing a Web page that makes a good contribution and benefits the lives of its visitors takes a little more time and effort. If a planned approach is adopted right from the start, the results can be worth waiting for. Let's look at some of the issues involved.

Establishing which elements to include

For a personal Home page, there's a wealth of information you can provide. You can establish what to put in your Web pages by answering two questions:

- Why are you providing a personal Web presence?

- Who is the Web page to be designed for – a section of the community or simply anyone?

As a general guide, also consider the following list:

- Your name and optionally any qualifications, letters, and so on, which you want to include. (If you have a long list of qualifications, arguably sometimes, a better impression can be created by including these more discreetly further 'down' your Web page, to avoid the possible misinterpretation of appearing pompous: remember, on a Home page, the first thirty seconds' impression makes a big impact)

...contd

- A good photograph of yourself – ideally not a passport-type photograph, but one which delivers a warmer impression or which meets the particular conditions you're trying to put over

- The first text paragraph is an ideal place to mention the purpose of your Web page. In this way, visitors who have mistakenly navigated to your site won't waste time (and clog up your site) by having to read further

- One way of providing an interesting focal point to your Web site is to build it around a theme. For example, you could describe your interests; or where you live; or your job, and so on

HANDY TIP

The Home or Introductory page is a good place in which to remind visitors to bookmark your site.

- If you want others to contact you, display essential contact information prominently. If you have several pages, perhaps include this information on each page

- Make sure visitors can easily navigate through your Web pages

- Above all, make it interesting; include lots of variety

This example is an excellent individual Web page design. Essential text hyperlinks are placed on the left and equivalent small graphic hyperlinks at the top for those browsers which can display them. Plus lots of active white space

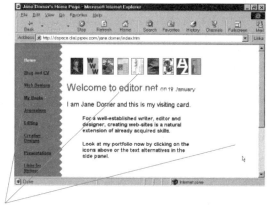

A Home page for doing business

If a traditional company has received positive press coverage, why not reference this information in a Web site. Respected independent praise can be a powerful sales aid.

The overriding aim of this type of Home page is to not only create new business but to help convert a prospect into a customer for as long as possible. This implies there's a need for periodic change and indeed this is true: updating a business-oriented Web site from time to time is *essential* to create an interesting, attractive and dynamic experience for visitors. In fact, that's the essence of a business page.

Avoiding reputation melt down

For businesses and organisations, the Home page is the online equivalent of the front door or corporate reception area. The impression created by a Home page is crucial to Web success. In fact, it could be argued that a poor or ill-considered corporate Home page can even damage an organisation's reputation quicker than most other ways.

People make judgements about the business by what they see (and possibly hear) on your Web pages, as well as what other people may say. It's crucial therefore, that a business oriented Web site must favourably reflect the image of the company or organisation and the branding of the products and services it represents.

For smaller companies or organisations, arguably, it's better not to give the impression of a large corporation. Web users will probably see through the fabrication eventually and credibility is then lost for ever. Instead, why not celebrate your uniqueness and build on it.

The power of a commercial Home page

The hyperlinks installed in a commercial Home page can provide the key to fast information access. A well thought out Home page can provide visitors with the means to make product comparisons and evaluations; check prices and place orders in minutes instead of hours or days. A Home page also acts like a signpost, guiding visitors to their desired part of your Web site. The pointers therefore, need to be clear, easy to use and direct.

However, one of the most striking characteristics of a Home page, is that your visitors always keep control. In a conventional sales presentation, only after the recipients have listened to the entire presentation, can they decide what is especially useful. Using the hyperlinks in a Home page, however, visitors can navigate to the areas that interest them almost immediately. This fact has powerful implications from a Web design standpoint.

...contd

HANDY TIP **Club- or business-oriented Web sites** often include a variety of Web pages. Navigation for visitors can be made easier by applying a frame-based design to the Home page and including an array of buttons.

BEWARE **Setting up an effective Web site** has got to be good for business. However, a poorly maintained Web site can pull the stature of an existing business down surprisingly quickly.

REMEMBER **Don't forget, to gain maximum** marketing advantage, you can apply the three most powerful words in advertising: YOU, NEW and FREE.

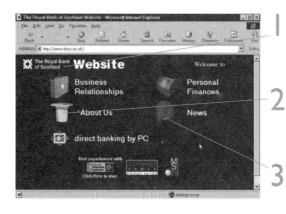

1 Logical positioning of essential branding element

2 Attractive graphics and good contrast with background

3 A news component to stimulate interest

Assessing the skills required

Let's look at the skills needed to create a successful corporate Web page. The key word to re-stress here is image. To create the correct Web image can involve some or all of the following IT skill-sets:

- A project manager responsible for getting the Web site up and running

- Graphic artists/designers who understand the peculiarities of graphic Web design

- HTML authors to produce the pages

- CGI programmers to design tailor-made Web forms

- Someone responsible for managing, maintaining and updating the Web pages

These skills may be available in-house, obtainable through contract workers, or you could contract the entire project to a dedicated Web page design consultancy.

Share a database and maximise exposure

It's possible to include all sorts of hyperlinks in a Web site. Of particular interest perhaps to corporate Web designers is the database connection: a Web page can include a link which allows a visitor to connect to a company's database to perform searches and to download relevant information.

Doing business: an activity checklist

For online stores in which inventory plays a key part, selling wares profitably is crucial to success. To get a better feel for what's involved in providing goods or services from a Web page design standpoint, let's take a brief look at a typical checklist covering the entire transaction process:

1 Research and establish the potential market for specific products and services

2 Create the design layout for all Web pages. *Remember, the design of the Home page is particularly important*

3 Create the entire text content for each Web page

4 Prepare the graphics and integrate with Web page designs. Possibly include multimedia and animation content

HANDY TIP

At any time, you can easily check out what's new on the Internet. Point your browser at: http:// www.whatsnew.com

5 Make it easy to carry out business transactions (for example: design dedicated online forms)

6 Set up a reliable, secure way to accept payment for goods or services (ideally use a secure server to process credit card transactions)

7 From the final designs, convert all content to HTML format

8 Publish pages to the Web

9 Make it easy for people to find your Home page (search engines, press releases, secondary advertising, etc.)

10 Dispatch the goods; carry out services

11 Devise methods which ensure you maintain in contact with customers on a regular basis

12 Periodically refresh interest in your Web pages: update existing pages to include new, fresh content. For example, perhaps include a 'What's New' page

This company simply and clearly demonstrates where their expertise lies with effective use of three buttons

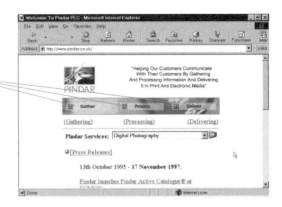

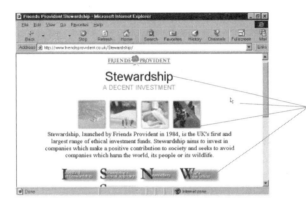

This company applies striking, soft-edged graphics, lots of white space and clean lines to demonstrate the essence of their offerings

The Ben & Jerry Home page is highly graphical and animated, tuning in perfectly to the whims of its visitor profile: our children

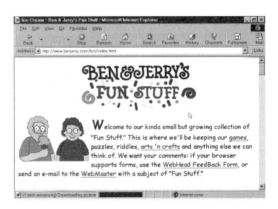

Deciding what to include

The following list includes some ideas of what you can include on a Home page:

- The title: individual, company or organisation name and the logo – essential for any organisation

- Traditional contact details: postal address, telephone and fax numbers; email and Web page addresses

- Copyright statement: essential to protect your work

 HANDY TIP

If you decide to include links to other companies and organisations on your Web pages, by placing these links at one dedicated location (page), you can reduce the risk of visitors leaving your Web site mistakenly.

- Clear index to the Web site. Perhaps a graphical toolbar-type design approach, or a 'looser' pictorial graphic design, or something entirely different. Whatever you choose, it's important to include a simple text equivalent of each graphic used

- All essential links to the other pages in the Web site: sales; catalogues; services; email response; and so on

- Links to relevant and thorough information about what you're offering (provide plenty of background information to support your case, but do so in such a way that visitors can choose whether to view it)

- If you want to provide a dedicated Web form page, ideally, include a link to it here

- Why not include something particularly relevant, eye-catching or stimulating to your visitors, and which can be changed or updated as desired. For example: perhaps an eye-catching 'What's New' or 'What's Hot' link could be useful here

- If relevant, why not include a brief company mission statement or a personalised quote from the managing director, chief executive or other leader

- Possibly include a link to some positive testimonials from satisfied customers – but get their written permission first

- A link pointing to job openings within the company

Encouraging visitors to return

HANDY TIP **If you're providing a Web site tour, the closing sequence is an ideal time to fire the imagination and prompt your visitors to action: perhaps to order a product or to revisit specific pages. Provide drama; make an impact and leave a lasting impression but most importantly, put over clearly the benefits you're providing.**

It's human nature to want to return to places we've visited in the past that were particularly enjoyable to us. Places like these immediately conjure up positive, cheerful, relaxed and carefree memories; long, lingering, hazy summer holidays at some exotic location for example. If you could create a similar, lasting impression with a Web page, you would soon be very successful. The point is, aim to create Web pages that are exciting and compelling to a carefully targeted audience.

Considering reasons why people might revisit

Whilst considering the overall design of your Home page, sometimes applying a little psychology is a useful exercise to help define your designs. Here are some reasons why a visitor might want to revisit a Web page:

- To gain something or to save money

- The Home page has been bookmarked in the visitor's browser. Always tell visitors to bookmark your page

- There's an interactive component: a link to an online game perhaps. Stimulating puzzles for example can also meet this condition

Stimulate visitors' imaginations with pleasing sights and sounds. Evoke the other sensations of touch and smell by drawing on memorable experiences. Relate your message with carefully crafted words. Spend as much time as you need to present your content well.

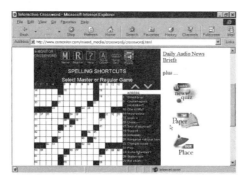

Web page crosswords or similar puzzles can help keep visitors online and interacting with your Web site

- To make the job of whatever it is they're doing, easier or to improve some aspect of their job or role

- The experience of visiting makes them feel good about themselves, by being invited to perhaps contribute in some way, or simply to help others

- The perception that the experience of visiting helps a visitor become a better person

- Memory of a page that is attractive and impressive

- They feel by visiting, they're in some way, taking part in something bigger; something more important than normal day to day activities

- The Web page is considered by peers to be the 'cool' place to visit

Maintaining the momentum

To make a Web page really work, it's not a bad idea to pretend that it's never finished. In other words, to encourage new visitors and prompt previous visitors to return, a Web site needs to be actively promoted and publicised regularly. Consider the following pointers to devise new ways to encourage visitors to return:

- Regularly look for ideas to generate schemes which you think would appeal to your visitors

- Find your visitors 'Hot' buttons. By that, I mean learn what they would really want from your Web site and try to provide it

- Try to find ways of interacting with previous visitors. For example: if you have previously obtained an individual's date of birth details, you could email a birthday congratulations several days before the event, with no strings attached, other than simply mentioning the Web page and inviting your customer to revisit. You could perhaps even include a mention of birthdays on the Web site; however consider this carefully, remember, some people may be sensitive about their age being revealed openly.

- Update a static Web site. Perhaps bring in multimedia-, Java-, and ActiveX-type components to help provide a fresh, new, exciting illusion of active content. Also, consider publishing genuine updates through traditional avenues, press releases, and so on.

Avoiding dead URL links

A dead URL link is a hypertext link to another Web address that no longer exists. Thousands of Web pages are being modified, updated, moved, reopened and closed each day. If you include links to other Web addresses in Web pages, before publishing your pages to the Web, make sure all such links are still correct. You can then make any changes necessary before publishing or updating your Web pages.

Also, once your Web site is active, it's a good idea to check the validity of any Web links you have included regularly, to avoid irritating your visitors with a 'This page can no longer be found' messages.

HANDY TIP

If you move your Web pages to another location, it's of course essential to ensure visitors know the new address. One remedy to this problem is to use the 'client pull' technique to automatically move visitors to your new site. Then mention the new address and invite visitors to bookmark it immediately. See your HTML guide for details.

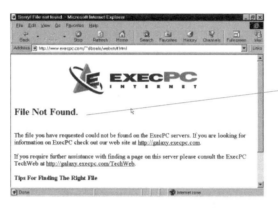

This is a situation you want to avoid at all costs. Make sure all your URLs are up-to-date and valid

This organisation has moved its Web pages. By including a linker page, they have ensured their visitors will reach the proper address

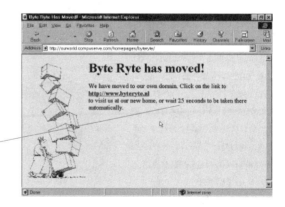

The email link

HANDY TIP

Another good way of connecting with visitors, is to include a link to a simple (optional) registration form page. Here, you could ask visitors to provide their basic contact details and particular areas of interest. Don't ask for too much information though: visitors may feel this is too intrusive.

Email is arguably one of the easiest ways in which the people you're trying to connect with can contact you. Although traditional contact methods like mail, phone and fax are easily available, an email facility is usually already set up on visitors' computers and is easily accessible. Consider other advantages:

- For businesses, sending an email costs a fraction of what it costs to send an equivalent letter

- An email can be in a recipient's mail box minutes later

- Most email systems now allow you to send not only text messages but standard application files – like databases, spreadsheets, and desktop published documents – as attachments to an email message

- Time zone differences become irrelevant. Recipients can collect email when it's convenient to them

- A recipient doesn't have to be present to receive email

- Where an email recipient lives becomes irrelevant

REMEMBER

Here's how email works. Each recipient 'rents' a storage area called an email box, on a powerful PC (mail server). The user can then periodically examine their email box and download any desired messages.

No wonder over 400 million email messages are sent across the globe each day. You can easily include an email link on your Home page and every other page in your Web site, by using the <A HREF= "MAILTO ...">...</A> HTML sequence. See your HTML guide for the exact syntax.

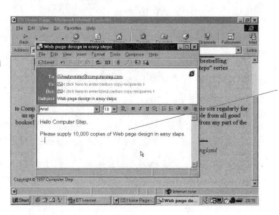

After a visitor clicks the MAILTO email link, the browser brings up the default email application window in which a user can compose and send an email

Creating an electronic signature

A 'signature' or electronic business card is a brief message – ideally under ten lines – which automatically accompanies any email message you send. Many email programs allow you to set up and attach a brief file signature in this way. You could include essential contact information, your name, postal address, telephone and fax numbers, email address and a striking sentence describing something important, relevant, or new. For example, as an author, I could include the following information:

Once you've created an electronic signature, often, you can set up your email application to automatically include the signature with every email you send.

> Brian Austin MISTC, computer author, trainer and IT support specialist.
> Email: B.Austin@btinternet.com
> Web page: http://www.SoftrightServices.co.uk

Creating a signature in Microsoft Outlook Express

In Microsoft Outlook Express – the accompanying email application for Microsoft Internet Explorer v4 – you can easily set up an email signature. You can start Outlook Express in Windows by clicking the Start button followed by Programs, then Internet Explorer, followed by Outlook Express.

Quite a few browsers include email utilities. But to provide more power and flexibility you can use a dedicated email application instead if you wish. For example, if you want more information, point your browser at: http://www. qualcomm.com and Pegasus Mail at: http://www. pegasus.usa.com

Alternatively, if you have Outlook Express set up as your default email program, with Internet Explorer 4 running, choose the Mail command on the Go menu. Then, with Outlook Express running as shown below, carry out the steps below and overleaf.

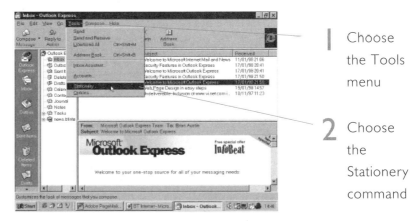

1 Choose the Tools menu

2 Choose the Stationery command

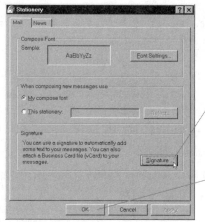

3 The Stationery dialog box appears. Click the Signature button

10 Click OK again to confirm your new settings

4 (Optional) Click here to place a tick mark if you want to include your signature with all outgoing emails

5 Now carry out either Step 6 or Step 7

6 If you want to enter a signature now, type it in this box. Then go to Step 9

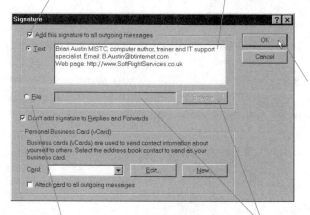

9 Click the OK button

7 If the text you want to use for your email signature is already in a file, click here

8 Click the Browse button, then navigate through the dialog boxes to select the file you want. Click the relevant OK buttons to place the name of your file in the box immediately to the left of the Browse button

Creating supplementary pages

Chapter Thirteen

If the Home page is like your front door, the supplementary pages are like the rooms in your house. Each of these pages may be designed to meet a specific need. Here, we look at essential and optional characteristics to consider when designing your supplementary pages.

Covers

Building a consistent approach | 140

Aim to dazzle your visitors | 142

Inform, amuse and entertain | 144

Making pages interactive | 146

Linking back to the Home page | 148

Establishing page length | 149

Dealing with related Web sites | 150

Building a consistent approach

When considering the design aspects of supplementary pages – that is, those which link back to the Home page – it's a good idea to consider having a consistent design style throughout all your pages.

Consistency across a series of Web pages helps reassure visitors in two ways:

Want to speed up the display of images used in your Web pages? Then simply use an image more than once. Most browsers store images in a cache after downloading. So if the same image is called on another Web page, the browser loads the cache image instead of downloading it a second time. Cache memory is much faster than downloading.

- An increased awareness that they're still on the same Web site

- Familiar signposts mean visitors can better establish their location within the scheme of things

The power of colours, styles and orientation

Colours can mean more than just colour. Why not consider a specific colour for page titles; another for subheadings, another for style of body text, and so on. This same colour scheme could be carried on to all your pages, so visitors know right from the outset what to expect. Another way in which you can help your visitors orient themselves is to place common design elements like logos, buttons, or other icons in the same place from page to page.

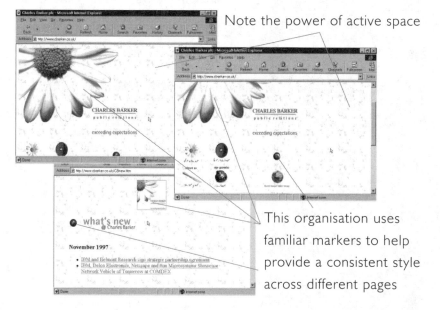

Note the power of active space

This organisation uses familiar markers to help provide a consistent style across different pages

Using a template

For larger Web sites containing many pages, often the easiest way to ensure consistency in design across all the pages is to create a design template which includes all the common text and graphic elements you want to include on every page. Here's how:

Avoid using too many different font styles. Ideally, keep to less than three unless you have a compelling reason to include four. Too many varying font styles can create a disjointed, 'ransom note' effect on a Web page.

1 First, establish all the components to include in your template

2 Next, create the template and save it

3 When you're ready to create a page based on the template, open the template and immediately save it to another name

4 You can then modify the page to include all the essential details for the current page, then re-save

5 Repeat Steps 3 and 4 for all the other pages you want to include

If possible, include navigation buttons, or their equivalent links, between the relevant Web pages. In this way, you can ensure your visitors don't have to rely on the Forward and Back buttons in their browsers.

From this sequence, it's easy to see how one single template design could make creating a series of pages like this much simpler

Using striking quotations stimulates interest, but do ensure such content does not in any way contradict what you're offering

Aim to dazzle your visitors

This section is all about trying to make a Web site appear not as a Web site, but as a stimulating experience! This might seem like an unlikely proposition, but there are Web sites out there doing just that. The essential fact is if your target visitors find your Web pages interesting, attractive and compelling, they're more likely to revisit and recommend them to others. If they revisit, you have further chances to state your case, start a dialogue, make a friend, or close a sale. And as any marketing guru should cite: personal recommendations are always best.

HANDY TIP

For any Web site to be a success, it needs to be actively promoted at every opportunity using the more conventional channels. Try to think of ways in which you can apply this advice to your needs.

Establishing what's appropriate

Page components however, should be appropriate for the type of audience visiting your Web page. Consider for example:

- Loud, visually bizarre components or similarly animated icons probably would not endear an audience logging on to a Web site devoted to fly fishing. Whereas carefully prepared images of the prize catches portraying the ones that 'didn't get away' in a backdrop of outstanding natural beauty certainly would be appreciated

- Taking this theme a little further, this kind of Web site could also include downloadable video sequences and fly fishing commentaries or sound effects, to further engage visitors' imaginations

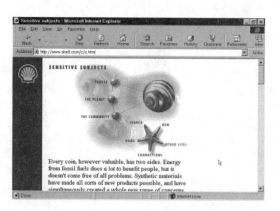

This organisation attempts to tackle head-on the issues which affect us all. By being open and not avoiding sensitive areas, such an approach can make a good impact

...contd

 When thinking about the design of your pages, take a look at what the competition are doing on their Web sites. This doesn't mean copy their content, but it does at least let you know what you've got to beat to 'steal their thunder'.

 Avoid using 'Under Construction' signs. Visitors may not take the providers of an unfinished page seriously, especially in business. If a page is not ready to put on the Web, arguably, it's more professional to complete its design entirely before uploading it to your Web site.

Helping visitors spread the word

If your visitors interact with your Web site positively and want to tell others, then your design efforts have proved to be correct and you have achieved an important objective.

You can build on this idea by doing some of this work for them: why not insert a special button or icon for visitors to click, which allows them to quickly insert the email address of someone they know who would also be interested in your site.

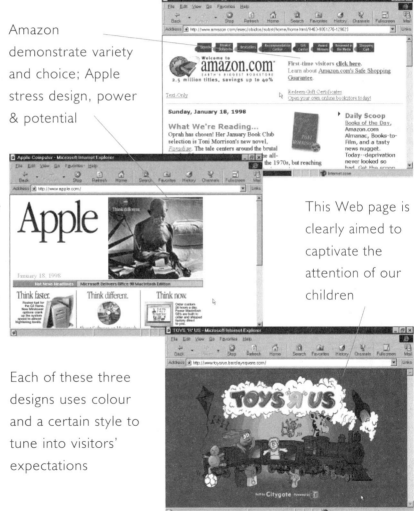

Amazon demonstrate variety and choice; Apple stress design, power & potential

This Web page is clearly aimed to captivate the attention of our children

Each of these three designs uses colour and a certain style to tune into visitors' expectations

Inform, amuse and entertain

Although images often provide an ideal presentation, make sure an image is not so large that it takes longer than about 25 seconds to download using a 28.8Kbps modem. After that amount of time, visitors may understandably become impatient and may decide to abort the visit.

For some users, Web pages can be likened to newsletters and brochures. As in these types of publications, images and other graphics play an important part. Often, an eye-catching graphic with its associated text one-liner can be the main ingredient which is designed to catch the visitor's eye. There's no reason why this technique cannot be applied to Web pages also; in fact, many powerful Web sites employ just this technique or a variation of it.

Using Humour

Jokes and cartoons, tastefully portrayed, can add final touches to a Web page – unless of course, you're in the laughter business – in which case, they can become the centrepiece of a Web site. Consider:

- To encourage feedback, you could try monthly joke contests with prizes – ideally products from the Web site – for the winners

- Or perhaps a competition to find the funniest, most unusual, or striking email address

Line art images – like cartoons – with a little colour included, can translate well onto a Web site. Line art images also compress easily and quickly. However, perhaps the most value from a Web design aspect is through their simplicity. Often, a simple, illustration stands out from the rest.

- Another idea successfully done recently, is to invite visitors to email in 50 words or less, why they think they deserve a free [product]. Then publish the results. I suspect some hilarious offerings could be forwarded in these situations offering high entertainment value to all concerned

Humour should be managed with no possibility of misinterpretation. Most people don't want to see gratuitous abuse of race, creed, religion, and so on

HANDY TIP For businesses, Instead of telling your visitors how your company can benefit them, why not show using examples or quoted testimonials from previously satisfied customers (but get permission first). Arguably, concrete, persuasive demonstration may achieve better results than simply delivering a sales talk.

HANDY TIP If you're selling a product or service, why not present brief details of the core subject, with access to lots of backup information using links. Provide this information in a clear, unbiased, sober and factual way using examples where possible.

Profiling Web page visitors for business

For anyone involved in selling goods and services over the Internet, arguably it's essential to try and learn more about Internet users – and for our purposes – particularly

Photo © ProMedia Software

Web users. People who purchase over the Web are still relatively unusual, and as such, deserve special consideration. Visitors who purchase online prefer to do so for several different reasons. Usually, online visitors:

- Like to keep control of the transaction

- Don't like the hard sell approach

- Don't appreciate uninvited sales attempts

- Prefer to have the choice whether to purchase and when they're ready

- Like to be assured they can change their mind without penalty

- Usually prefer to have access to plenty of relevant background information

- May not appreciate online junk mail

Running in the background

You can alter the ambience a Web site has to offer by running complimentary events in the background; for example: RealAudio technology can be applied here to include appropriate sound files.

However, if you decide to follow this route, it's a good idea to periodically assess whether the background content gets in the way of the main message of the page, possibly causing confusion.

Making pages interactive

Even though visitors to your Web pages can communicate simply by viewing your pages, your interaction with visitors need not be limited to just this way. The Internet is a two-way system, with several levels of interactivity possible. However, in the context of the Web, it's especially important that you respond quickly and efficiently to any enquiry: visitors can't usually see (yet) who they're connecting with, and so a quick response is especially important. One way to do this is to set up an infobot system. Remember, an infobot is essentially an automated email fax-back system. You can use infobots to provide an automatic response to Web page enquiries received by email. To ensure your respondents have confidence in your infobot system, let's recap and consider the following points:

HANDY TIP

Some ISPs only host Web sites and don't provide any dial-up services. However, for promoting a serious Web presence, these may provide a good choice. Shop around, compare offerings. The better Web host providers also provide autoresponders/infobots. You can then design as many autoresponses as you need to automate much of the general enquiry-type communications. This approach frees you to concentrate your prime time on more profitable ventures.

- It's important to respond to emails quickly and efficiently

- The responding infobot can provide a valuable time-saving element for you by being designed on a FAQ (Frequently Asked Questions) list basis

- In this way you can quickly ensure most of the enquirers' questions are answered properly. In fact, a proper response is vital to build a working, trustful relationship with enquirers and to convert those enquirers to customers, if that is your aim

- The way in which these responses are dealt with can forge the basis for a profitable relationship from day one. Customers left with a favourable impression is one of the best advertisement for any business or organisation

The value of contests

Many of us enjoy competitions. But even if we're not competitive, most of us like to have a chance at winning a prize. Providing contests in a Web site adds special value. Consider the points below in relation to your Web pages:

- Contests can urge people to want to visit your Web site and if managed properly, to revisit continually

- You could aim to integrate your products and services as part of a contest. In the 'Who did it' style, you could spread clues throughout your Web site to encourage visitors to view the offerings, almost subconsciously. In this way visitors take the fast track to learn about what's on offer – there can also be greater potential for more sales here

- Contest participants need to provide information about themselves. In fact, this is one of the main reasons for hosting a contest in the first place. This information, if managed creatively and actively, is of utmost importance. The Web for all its colour, glamour and activity can be like a dark room: unless someone shouts their name, you don't know they're present. Anything that encourages visitors to say 'Hello, I'm here; this is who I am', has real value

Anything new on your Web site, whether it be a contest, new product range or service could also be promoted further using traditional means like press releases, brochures, and so on.

Here, contests form central elements of the page

Linking back to the Home page

After navigating six or seven 'hops' from your Home page, a visitor would not appreciate having to backtrack the same way to return to your Home page. Therefore, unless you have a compelling reason not to do so, it's always a good idea to include a link back to your Home page on all other pages in your Web site.

This also provides visitors with a standard point of reference: if they get lost, they know how to get back to 'the beginning' with a single click.

HANDY TIP

While viewing a page in your Web site, a visitor may suddenly decide they want to contact you. You could make it easy for them to do this by including a link to your 'Contacts' page or section on every page in your Web site.

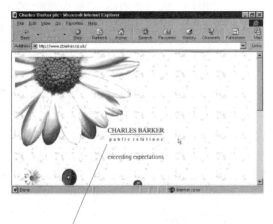

This Home page has limited content, rather it puts emphasis on impact and design. Often however, Home pages contain essential content

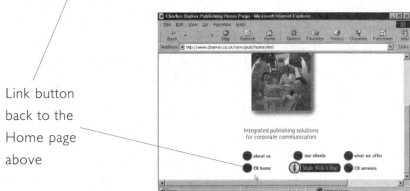

Link button back to the Home page above

Establishing page length

An admirable objective is to try to install all text, graphics, pictures and animation-type components within the physical space of one screen. This ensures visitors don't have to scroll through to find the desired information.

Providing index headers for a longer Web page

Including everything on one screen though is not always possible – or desirable. However, the one-screen approach probably works best for individuals, and smaller companies or organisations who perhaps provide only one or two products or services. In this scenario, it can make sense to put everything on one carefully designed scrollable page, with index pointers included at the top or start of the Web page.

Results of research into Web page users has confirmed that generally people don't like to scroll. However, perhaps the key point here is incentive: if visitors perceive the benefits, providing not too much scrolling is called for, most people would tolerate some scrolling.

An index pointer is simply any text or graphic link which when clicked, takes the visitor to the corresponding part of the page – again, ideally providing all the relevant information for that section within one screen. The main

point about this approach, is that you can minimise the number of times a visitor has to click on the scroll buttons. This approach can work well for predominantly information providing Web sites, for example, as in the ScreenThemes Web page picture above. Carefully placed at the bottom of these screens of information, you could also include a link back to the index at the top of the page.

One way to help ensure your Web pages display within an acceptable time, is to try and ensure the text content on each page is limited to no more than about 600 words.

If your design plan means index pointers aren't appropriate, as long as the reasons to scroll are clear and incentives are present, most visitors will accept this approach. For larger companies providing perhaps thousands of product lines, long Web pages are usually the best and often the only practical option.

Dealing with related Web sites

Providing a link to other Web sites, might not, at first, seem like an effective way of enhancing your own Web page. However, it can work. Here's how.

The Web is expanding at an incredible rate with new pages coming online every day. If you're serious about including links to other sites, one of the fastest ways to find new, relevant sites, is to regularly use the search engines to do the job for you. Think global, not local. Distance is not usually relevant on the Web.

Let's assume you provide a Web site selling books. You could include a link to another online store which primarily sells videos and music CDs. So for example, if a music celebrity has just published their sizzling autobiography, after customers have placed their book order on the dedicated Web form, they could also easily gain access to our celebrity's most popular videos and CDs simply by clicking the associated link.

Customers benefit by having access to a better service and quick access to related subjects should they choose to follow these up. Likewise, the video Web site provider could include a complementary link to the bookseller's Home page. In this way, both providers can benefit from new visitors. Here's one way to do it:

Three or more Web sites could even work together to provide special deals for customers and to help boost their own individual product sales.

1   Note the names of complimentary companies and organisations which you would like to associate with. The search engines can be useful here to find exact Web addresses

2   Log on to each of these chosen sites and send a brief email to the Webmaster at each address introducing yourself, your Web site and your proposal. Most important, mention your Web site address. Also mention that in return for them including a link to your Web site, you will include a link to theirs. Now wait for a reply

3   If agreement has been reached and written (emailed) permission given you can include an eye-catching attractive link either in a dedicated 'Other links' page, or at an appropriate location on your Home page

Designing Web pages for marketing

Marketing is arguably one of the most powerful reasons why the Web has grown at such a fast pace. The business of advertising is central to the Web. But the Web is like no other advertising medium and as such deserves careful and special consideration. In this chapter, we tackle these and other related issues.

Covers

Establishing your marketing goals | 152

The two-step design plan | 153

Standing out | 154

Advertising on the Web | 155

Adding extra value | 156

Creating a visitor's experience | 158

Using newsgroups | 160

Using mailing lists | 161

Providing FAQ lists | 162

Chapter Fourteen

Establishing your marketing goals

Businesses, clubs and organisations can have various reasons for deciding to extend marketing operations to a Web site. However, at the outset of the Web project, it's important to identify what you hope to gain through marketing online. The goals you highlight should then determine the message content in your Web pages.

Reassessing your uniqueness

When defining Web page marketing goals, it's often an ideal time to reassess and re-examine the qualities that make your business, club, or organisation unique. In this way, you can hopefully develop a more focused approach to creating an online marketing plan, as covered on the following page.

The Web provides access to an incredible amount of useful marketing and research information for businesses. The trick however, to save time and maintain your sanity, is to filter out the irrelevant information. It pays to learn as much as possible about using search engines, online business directories, and so on.

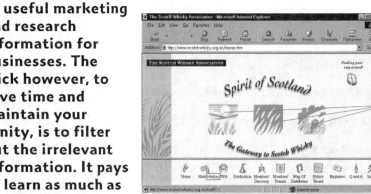

The Scotch Whisky Association Home page displays a proud style that echoes its products. Three simple graphics and a striking colour scheme effectively put over the link with the land

Reducing marketing costs

Generally, most marketing experts would agree that it's much easier to sell new products and services to an existing customer, than to foster a new customer. Use of the Internet can make the business of communicating with existing customers easier and cheaper.

When true costs are worked out, using the telephone is clearly much cheaper than sending a letter. But sending an email is cheaper still: one reason why over 400 million emails are sent across the globe each day. Therefore, why not try to integrate email communications closely with your Web page designs to benefit fully from these cost savings.

The two-step design plan

Effective Web pages can be created in many ways, however, often, you can make the job easier by constructing and following a basic plan. For example, why not:

1 Create your Web site with quality as the criteria above all else in mind. Aim for *quality* in all aspects and especially in your information and its presentation

2 Then, look for ways in which you can *add extra value*, but make sure these are tangible; something that really matters to your potential customers

BEWARE

If you're in the business of providing advice, it's a good idea to have professional indemnity insurance to cover yourself against any possible chance of being sued. Remember, the Web is a global medium and therefore legal repercussions may not be clear.

Step 1 above is self-evident and is achieved simply through care, consideration and plenty of testing. Real world examples for meeting the Step 2 condition are covered in more detail on page 156 of this chapter. However, other ideas for Step 2 could include the following:

- Create a virtual hook by providing free information or advice which is valuable to the target audience

- Including plenty of options for customer feedback

- A page introducing 'What's New'

- Provide a link to the company newsletter

- Maybe include a separate table of contents page (however, this can have obvious disadvantages)

This Web site makes available a screensaver for download free of charge. The key point is that the screensaver is a quality product in its own right and includes only subtle advertising

Standing out

Once you've clearly established your marketing goals and developed a plan, consider the following ideas to help make your Web pages stand out:

Humour can be a powerful tool in the hands of a careful and considerate Web designer. Fun has its own reward. If we create a fun time on a Web site, it becomes compelling and the mood is set for revisits and further developments.

- Create attractive marketing content that is appropriate for your Web pages

- Experiment with ideas to describe your products and services in a compelling and eye-catching way

- As with desktop publishing, sometimes empty space on a Web page can work for you – in fact, this type of empty space could be perhaps better renamed active space

- Although lots of attention-seeking components are available, sometimes a clean, uncluttered Web page can carry its own message

For advertisers and marketing providers, multimedia content – the combining of text, graphics, animation, video and sound – in a Web site can be considered as one of the most powerful approaches in progressive advertising.

Sometimes, considered design containing white (active) space can help key components stand out, just as effectively as using bright colours or applying animation techniques

Assessing the competition

Designing a Web page to stand out from the crowd requires that you know just what the 'crowd' is doing on 'their' Web sites. Therefore, it's a good idea to get hold of a list of competitors' Web sites, start up your Web browser and see how the competition approaches this aspect:

- Note down the kind of Web page components that gain your attention and try to define why

- Also, note down those components and elements that irritate you or cause problems for your browser. This kind of information could be useful in establishing what not to include in your own Web pages

Advertising on the Web

The Web is an ideal advertising medium. The cost of advertising through a Web page is small compared to conventional media. Also, unlike conventional advertising channels like magazines, newspapers and television, advertising space on the Web is not in short supply (yet). This allows for a wide scope, providing many opportunities for including a vast range of information at low cost. Web advertisers can better focus their message to effectively reach such target groups as:

- Information seekers

- Individuals who are cost conscious

- Number seekers: those who benefit from viewing statistics, graphs and charts

- People who are more likely to be motivated to action through a graphically rich Web design environment

- Those who are first and foremost quality conscious and value oriented

- People who particularly enjoy audiovisual content

- And so on

HANDY TIP

Ezines – Internet magazines – can provide another valuable advertising source. Usually, it's best to stick with those providers who email their ezine only to people who have specifically requested it (non-spam). The cost of advertising in these types of publication is low and often worthwhile. Also, there are hundreds of ezine sources on the Net that may include your advert for free.

Advertising approaches

If you want to attract a visitor's attention to perhaps 'pull the visitor in' to an advertisement, one technique that can work is to employ some kind of animation or movement embedded within an eye-catching colour scheme.

Another approach is to try and create interest out of the mundane. One way this can be done is to pull in related items or subject matters and tie these in with a Web page.

The importance of branding on the Web

To advertise successfully on the Web, many experts agree that a strong brand name promoted equally strongly on the Web pages, provides one of the most essential ingredients for achieving a successful Web trading experience.

Adding extra value

Designing a good Web page is a worthwhile achievement. However, creating an effective Web page should be the preferred aim. To entice visitors to log on to a Web page *and* to keep them coming back repeatedly requires a special kind of thinking. Firstly, when visitors log on to a Web site, remember they're spending in three ways:

- Time needed to visit a Web site

- Time lost through not performing other activities whilst online

- The cost involved in setting up a Web browser and in maintaining an Internet link (online costs)

Visitors therefore, must perceive to be getting value from their Web surfing investment. One way to meet this need is to be perceived as providing extra value to the Web page visitor.

Providing added value to a Web site

You can build a generic Web page and then modify it for a desired purpose. Or you could design for a specific purpose right from the start. In Step 2 of the two-step design plan on page 153, here are some real-world examples:

- An online music store could provide some free downloads (note: copyright issues would have to be resolved)

- A bookstore could give away a free choice of book up to a certain value, when a customer places an order above a specific quantity or order value

- A market research company could provide some free information that is valuable to Web page respondents

- A consultant could provide a free information sheet covering key advice and information on specific topics. This could be included on a Web page or sent to Web page respondents when they send in their contact details *and* a specific code (the consultant then knows this code relates only to the Web page)

HANDY TIP

When a visitor is viewing a page and then clicks a link to another section or another Web address, usually the target section or new Web page is immediately displayed. However, new techniques are emerging which allow a designer to cause a variety of transitions to take place. For example: zooming, fading, panning, and even new types of pop-up windows are now possible.

- An accountancy Web site could provide some free information on a range of topics. Perhaps change the topic once weekly/monthly to heighten interest

- Press releases could be provided at strategic times giving up-to-the minute information on new products, services or developments which might be of interest to customers. And so on

When providing extra value components, to achieve maximum effect, positioning can be important. One of the most powerful positions is the uppermost left corner of the screen, as our eyes are naturally drawn to this location at first glance.

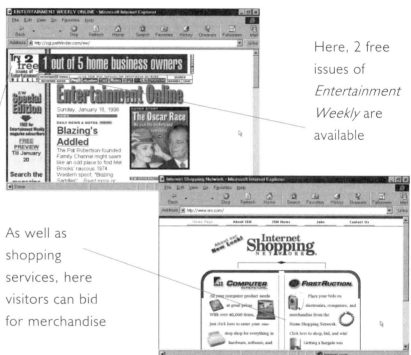

Here, 2 free issues of *Entertainment Weekly* are available

As well as shopping services, here visitors can bid for merchandise

Make it easy for visitors to contact your Web site and place an order

Although you can include a simple email link in your Web pages, you can ensure the process of contacting a Web site and ordering products and services is made even easier for your visitors. In addition to providing essential traditional contact details, for businesses involved in supplying products, it's a good idea to include a link to a specially prepared order form on every page.

Creating a visitor's experience

By thinking of a Web page visit in terms of a visitor's experience, rather than purely a visual event, we can change our thinking so that the design we create can enhance these events for visitors.

Identifying with familiar universal things

Instead of thinking of the design of a Web page as simply pictures and text, why not approach the job differently using sensory association – *link the content of your Web pages closely to the human senses of sight, touch, smell, hearing and speech.* Consider the following example.

HANDY TIP

In the context of Web page text content, showing how or why something is the way it is, is much better than simply telling someone it's better. In this way, you're stating your case with evidence instead of simply delivering an online speech.

Let's assume you work for a confectionery food manufacturer and are responsible for outlining the design of the forthcoming Web pages. The page you're currently working on is about a new kind of chocolate. Perhaps you could borrow techniques from how you might make a conventional presentation of this new kind of chocolate: using videos, sounds, smells, evocative and seductive phrases, and so on.

Perhaps you might start by zooming in to a mouthwatering image of this new chocolate, with a brief but carefully worded paragraph stating all that is exciting about this particular flavour. You could include a video play button showing how the chocolate is made or perhaps a short television-type advertisement.

HANDY TIP

Above all, I would argue that visitors respond to: quality products, quality services, and reliable, unbiased information.

Below you could address different issues by providing key information. Some of your visitors might want to know about the calorie count; the ingredients used; the other flavours available, and so on, so why not provide links to other pages providing this information.

In this way, you can achieve an amazing balance in two ways:

- Firstly, you're advertising so there's a *persuasion element* linked to 'telling' and coaxing the visitor

- Secondly, by providing unbiased, reliable information, your *showing, not telling*

Here's a list of ten key words I would associate with any successful Web page: convincing, energising, interesting, absorbing, fascinating, compelling, unique, valuable, useful, and easy.

Writing the text content for an advertising-related Web page can involve much writing and rewriting to avoid presenting an overblown offering. However, your efforts could result in a superb sequence of lean, top quality, visitor-friendly Web pages.

Watch the text that is 'as smooth as silk'

One of the key aspects to creating the text content for this kind of Web page is the importance of the words used and how they could identify with the senses and evoke memories that are familiar to people. The golden rule here is to say your piece clearly and simply without overloading the piece with too many adjectives and waffle. We need to know the limit on how far we can stretch this approach: too much association and we risk sounding ridiculous. Consider the following imaginary example, which in my opinion is excessively overblown:

> 'Chocolate Nectar is our newest product. Its smooth, mouthwatering texture glides down the throat like a ... [first comparison, I can almost hear the visitor sighing] ... while the delicious taste lingers and tantalises your taste buds like ... [arguably, another yawning comparison]'

Many Web page visitors would have 'switched off' at the end of the second sentence. Often, simplicity works!

Why people buy over the Web

People buy from a Web store for many reasons, however, often there's one important reason above all others which affects their buying decision. From a Web page design standpoint, we could benefit by identifying some of the more important reasons why people buy from a Web store. Consider the following list:

- The four favourites: price, quality, branding and usefulness

- Perceived value

- Some people can be simply so entranced by a Web site presentation, that they decide to buy simply as a result of a mood created by their visit

If you can meet that last condition in the list above, you'll no doubt be envied by peers and competitors alike – perhaps understandably, it's the hardest one to achieve.

Using newsgroups

Be careful with advertising in newsgroups. A little discreet advertising is usually tolerated as long as a genuine contribution is being made; usually this means providing some useful and possibly valuable information to the group. See note on netiquette in Chapter 1, page 15.

Well over 20,000 newsgroups are usually available covering hundreds of different themes. If you're considering posting an article, make up a list of all the relevant newsgroups. You can usually download all the titles to see what's available from your Internet Service Provider. Contact your ISP for more details.

A newsgroup is a computer-based storage area containing a collection of articles or posted messages on a particular topic. Newsgroups can be accessed through an Internet Service Provider or through a direct connection to the Internet. There can be thousands of different newsgroups covering hundreds of different topics. Anyone can post to a newsgroup and anyone can read newsgroup postings.

People contributing to newsgroups give up their time and information freely, in the hope that they too will learn from others. Therefore, it's important to note that people visiting newsgroups don't expect to see much evidence of commercial activity. In fact, for many people, this is one reason for visiting: to discover true information and genuine opinions, not those based on commercial self-interest.

Having said that, many companies and organisations do break the unwritten rules. Sometimes, this can invite more problems for the 'unofficial law breaker' than it solves. Nevertheless, some unobtrusive advertising may be tolerated as long as it's discreet, brief and to the point, and perhaps most importantly, contributes in some way to the general theme of the newsgroup.

Posting messages to the newsgroups

To get the best from the newsgroups, you could try carrying out the following procedure:

1. Design an appropriate message: keep it simple, brief and to the point. Above all, make a useful contribution

2. Post your message in all the *relevant* newsgroups. Don't send your message to more than five newsgroups at any one time; if the newsgroups become saturated, your message may become lost and recipients may become irritated by the excessive repetition (spamming). You can find out about the range of newsgroups available from your Internet Service Provider.

Using mailing lists

A mailing list is exactly what it says. Putting your email address on any of the thousands of mailing lists covering as many topics, is the quickest way to receive a lot of email.

For a business or anyone wanting to sell goods and services on a regular basis, don't consider mailing lists to be your main avenue of business. Mailing list contributors can react very negatively against those blatantly carrying out 'excessive' commercial activities.

Although no laws exist to stop companies advertising in the mailing lists, a lot of grief can be avoided by respecting the right to privacy of individuals against excessive commercialism. Although mailing lists are not really designed with commerce in mind, brief commercial details included at the end of a useful message are usually tolerated, provided these details are discreet.

Also, if the contribution received by the participants in the list is perceived to be especially valuable and worthwhile, news about such contributions can be spread quite quickly. In this scenario, carefully crafted email signatures can reap benefits far in excess of the amount of input required to create them.

You can find mailing lists using the Internet search engines and at mailing list directory sites such as: http://www.reference.com

Taking part in newsgroups and mailing lists, on a regular basis, can help generate important contacts and valuable referrals.

What is true for newsgroups is also true for mailing lists. Here again, people give their time and information freely. As a result, many people can benefit from others' experiences freely.

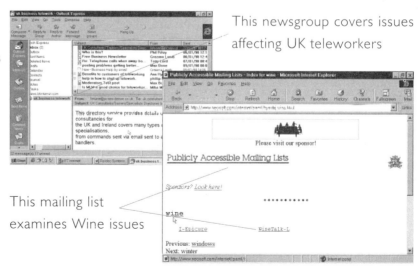

This newsgroup covers issues affecting UK teleworkers

This mailing list examines Wine issues

Providing FAQ lists

People buying products and services may have many questions to ask before making the decision to buy. If you're designing a Web site that includes some level of customer support, sometimes a single Web page dedicated to answering Frequently Asked Questions (FAQs) can be a valuable aid for your visitors whilst saving you a lot of extra work.

Some of the benefits of providing FAQ files include:

Microsoft's *FrontPage* is one example of Web page design software which includes a template Wizard to help design a FAQ Web page. Wizards to help design other Web pages: like those to provide press releases and glossary of terms are also included in this package.

- They can overcome possible objections to a sale without requiring direct contact (instant cost saving)

- Demonstrates consideration has been given to customers' needs in detail right from the outset

- They can provide a greater range of information enabling customers to make better buying decisions

- They can reduce the need for after-sales problem-solving support as basic questions can be answered in advance

To create a FAQ list, follow the steps below:

If you can provide FAQ lists, usually it's a good idea to do so. The cost of Web space, compared with more traditional advertising media is low and so this method offers real value for money.

1 Think of as many common questions people might ask and then clearly document both the questions with the answers. If, during this exercise, other possible questions emerge, don't worry, by providing the answers, you're actually making the buying decision easier for your customers

2 If necessary, interview sales and support staff who regularly deal with these kinds of problems to learn about the kind of questions visitors might ask

3 Save, edit, check and convert the FAQ file to HTML format and include with your Web site

4 Provide a link to the FAQ file, possibly on the Home page and maybe other appropriate pages too. Make sure visitors know about your FAQ pages

Gaining information with online forms

A Web form is simply the online equivalent of a paper-based form. Just like paper-based forms, we can love them or hate them. However, Web forms can open the door to a source of valuable information that Web site providers could not otherwise gain. Perhaps more importantly, these forms can enable Web transactions to take place faster and more efficiently. Let's look at the issues involved in providing Web forms.

Chapter Fifteen

Covers

Why use a Web form? | 164

How Web forms work | 165

Web form building blocks | 166

Security issues | 168

Some design hints and tips | 169

Example Web forms | 170

Why use a Web form?

A form can be a powerful aid as it can enable three important actions to take place on a Web page:

- Interactivity: a form allows a user to interact directly with a Web page

- Valuable user-related information can be gathered

- Collected information can be processed and returned to the Web page provider, usually by automated email

For businesses, this means web page forms can fulfil two main conditions or requirements:

- Gather all kinds of information. The right kind of information – particularly marketing information – is so important that it can be considered as a sort of global currency

- Receive focused feedback about goods or services

If you want to include forms in your Web pages, check with your Internet Service Provider which services and scripts they provide for processing forms.

You can of course, use a simple email link to meet both of the above requirements, and for many Web page providers this approach may be adequate for their needs.

However, carefully designed forms take the load of visitors and can deliver much more focused information. To make full use of raw emailed information, you would have to extract the essential points, categorise them and enter the information elsewhere, probably using yet further software tools. Using of a form however, can automate this process and make the task much easier.

The use of forms for processing Web transactions is also becoming commonplace now that Internet users are becoming more relaxed about leaving sensitive information like credit card details online using secure servers (see Chapter 16 for more information).

How Web forms work

REMEMBER

The Web forms server is either located at your Internet Service Provider's premises, or if you're hosting your own Web site, directly on one of your own powerful PCs designated for the job.

REMEMBER

A CGI script is a computer program which completes a task or series of tasks and which ignores any outside intervention.

HANDY TIP

CGI scripts can also be used to carry out a range of other valuable tasks on a Web page. For example: fast-changing data such as stocks and shares can be displayed and updated on-the-fly. For more information, speak to your ISP or CGI-programmer.

Forms became possible in Web pages with the introduction of the HTML v2.0 standard. All Web forms have two main components:

- The visible part in which we enter information into a variety of edit- or selection-type boxes

- The invisible component which deals with the processing of the entered information. Usually, this is done using a special process and language called a CGI (Common Gateway Interface) script

Once a visitor has completed entering information in a Web page form and clicked the Submit or Send button, the information is sent, stored and processed on the Web forms server usually by following the instructions in the CGI script. CGI usually establishes two things:

- How information entered in a Web form is routed first to the Forms server (a powerful PC)

- How the resulting information is routed back to the user's Web browser for confirmation

Scripting options

Some Internet Service Providers support various kinds of Web form processing scripts as part of their standard service. The well known Internet Service Provider, Demon, for example, supports at least four basic types of script: forms processing, forms test script, page counter, and clickable graphics. With other ISPs, you can pay for these extra services. Note, some ISPs may not support any scripting services.

A script can be written in a variety of computer languages, however, as scripts are hosted on an ISP's server computers, many ISPs already offer script writing services. Alternatively, you can make arrangements to provide your own script which meets your ISP's criteria. Whichever route you choose, it's important for the script writer to liaise closely with your Internet Service Provider when creating scripts.

Web form building blocks

Web forms design can be simple or complex. The more complex a form, the more finely-tuned the response can be, providing precise rather than vague information.

All Web forms are made up of simple elements or building blocks; the most common of these include:

- Text entry boxes: these allow a defined amount of text to be entered; password-type boxes can also come under this category

- Hidden fields: these are similar to a text entry box, except each character entered is displayed as an asterisk (*) to hide sensitive information from prying eyes

- Check boxes: these indicate one or more chosen options. A check box can be on (box ticked) or off (box clear). More than one check box can be made active at any one time

- Radio buttons: here only one of several options can be chosen. When one radio button is turned on, the HTML ensures all others in the related group are turned off automatically

- Pop-up menus and scrolling menus: provide menu choices either as a fully displayed block or as multiple options made available through a scrollable list

- Plain push-buttons: include two basic HTML types: SUBMIT sends all data in a form to the server. RESET usually clears the form by entering default values in each field in the form (these buttons can be given different names, like those shown in the Railtrack search page shown opposite)

- Image push-buttons – here a graphic- or image-type icon can be used instead of the plain grey-type box as described in the previous item

Radio button
(option button)

Text entry box (plain)

Text entry box (with
scroll bar)

**A Web
page form
need not
be plain in
appearance. If you
have a series of Web
pages constructed
using a template,
you may want to
maintain continuity
and so can include
strong branding
components or even
advertisements.
However, you need
to balance the
benefits against the
possible drawback
of making a form
too 'busy'.**

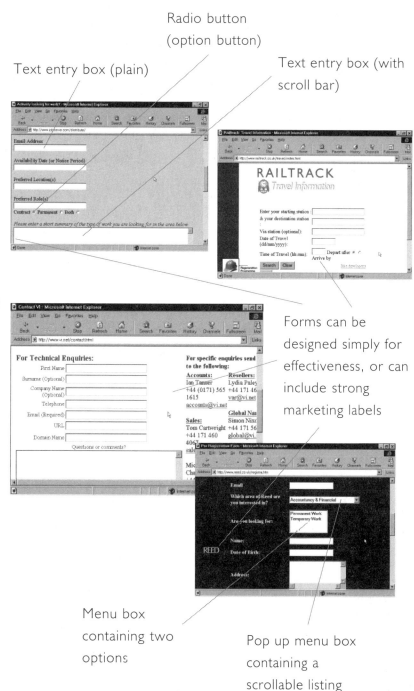

Forms can be
designed simply for
effectiveness, or can
include strong
marketing labels

Menu box
containing two
options

Pop up menu box
containing a
scrollable listing

Security issues

To keep things simple, it's possible to set up a Web page form to send its information using email. However, this does mean the information is not as secure when compared to using a CGI script. So don't use this method when dealing with sensitive data.

The business of transmitting sensitive information like credit card details over the Internet and the Web has been given a massive boost recently by the popular application of secure servers. Results of relevant statistics and the words of the many reputable authorities addressing the problem point to the almost undeniable fact that Internet order processing is now probably one of the safer ways through which to pay for goods and services, *providing* the seller uses a secure server to carry out the transaction.

When conventional credit card transactions take place in say a restaurant or retail store, unscrupulous individuals can simply listen carefully and look over the payee's shoulder to gain quite a lot of useful information; not so with a secure server! The use of secure servers is covered in more depth in Chapter 16.

Computer viruses can be hidden in attach-ments to email files, such as those in Microsoft Word and Excel files containing macros or pure binary programs (files ending with .exe or .com). If you're hosting a Web presence directly, rather than through a provider, use the most up-to-date antivirus software to help stay virus-free.

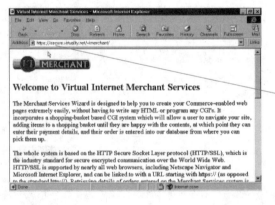

Virtual Internet's secure server identification. Note the 's' (for secure server) attached to 'http' label, to form https://

If you want to restrict access to some of your Web pages, user name and password fields can offer an effective solution

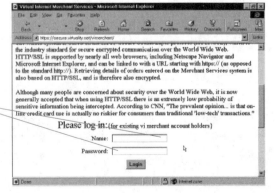

Some design hints and tips

When designing a Web form, in some ways it's a little like working blind: you don't know for example, about the capabilities of a particular visitor's computer system; the browser they're using; which fonts are installed, and so on. However, by talking to others who have successfully created forms and applying the guidelines in this book and similar sources, you can produce a working solution and avoid the pitfalls. Consider the following points:

- You can include commands in HTML to create several separate forms, in which each is capable of collecting and sending distinct information to the server. However remember, this approach can confuse visitors and is therefore, probably best avoided, unless you have a compelling reason to include multiple forms in this manner

- Once a form has been designed, test it using as many different Web browsers as possible to ensure maximum compatibility

- Often, you can easily set up a form to deal with simple enquiries or to obtain feedback from your Web page visitors. What's more, the chances are, your ISP may already have a form script designed to meet your needs. The only modification you may need to make might be to enter the email address to which you want the gathered information to be sent

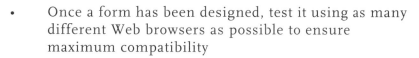

BEWARE

It's possible to include a separate form 'inside' another. However, nesting forms in this way can often lead to confusion and so is usually best avoided unless you have a compelling reason to insist on this approach.

Computer Step's Web site customer feedback form. In this type of form, remember, the largest edit box is reserved for customer comments

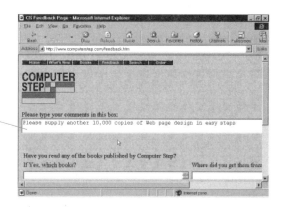

Example Web forms

The forms on this page are from Virtual Internet Limited. Their Wizard approach empowers anyone to set up an online shop easily

HANDY TIP

The Virtual Internet 'Wizard' approach to creating an online shop or store, is examined in more depth in the following chapter. This question and answer approach makes the job simple for anyone who doesn't want to get involved with programming, but would rather spend time promoting their business.

Here, you can choose whether to insert a company logo or a company name

The finished product: an example of how any business can display and sell their wares using a Web page

Designing Web pages to accept orders

Selling goods and services on the Web can be more profitable than using traditional channels. A bold statement, but to be effective this often requires a special approach. This chapter examines the options available to help make those all-important sales and some things to consider when designing these special Web pages.

Covers

Providing a secure server | 172

Using simple email forms | 173

Traditional contact information | 174

Designing a Web page order form | 175

Setting up shop the Wizard way | 177

Getting paid | 179

Chapter Sixteen

Providing a secure server

In Netscape Navigator, to tell if you're connecting through a secure server, look at the key icon situated at the lower left of the screen. This key appears in unbroken blue for secured connections and broken blue for unsecured links.

When sending sensitive information over the Internet, if you are unsure of security, check these aspects with the Webmaster before transacting.

To easily identify a secure server, look at the Web address. If there 's an 's' as in https://, the link is secure. Ordinary Web addresses start with: http://

What exactly is a secure server?

Don't be intimidated by the term secure server. Think of a server simply as a powerful PC which serves other PCs in some way. The 'secure' description, simply implies that information moving between the central server and the PCs it serves, is protected in some way: usually this is done by encrypting the information to prevent unauthorised access.

Why bother providing a secure server?

When sensitive information like credit card details are being transferred across the Internet without any protection, it's possible for unscrupulous people to copy that information and use it to steal from the unfortunate credit card holder's account. In this event, usually most credit card companies would claim the holder must have given their details and are therefore liable for the costs. However, using a secure server for carrying out Web transactions usually offers a much safer alternative. Statistically, it's now considered by many as safer to transmit credit card details over the Internet using a secure server, than to use a credit card in person in a high street shop, restaurant or garage.

Protecting privacy with encryption technology

Many secure servers use the Secure Sockets Layer (SSL) system. SSL is an encryption technology which is available on the Microsoft Windows and Apple Mac platforms. It's a method that has actually been available since the earlier versions of Netscape Navigator and Internet Explorer.

For the technically minded, the SSL system can use a 128-bit encryption key for US transactions and a 40-bit key for international transactions. To break the 40-bit code, using a powerful 200MHz Pentium PC working continuously 24 hours a day, would take between 1-2 years of processor time, so says one reputable estimate. A more determined thief using a network of hundreds of PCs could perhaps break the code in several weeks. However, each exchange of data uses a different key, so breaking one key would not help our imaginary thief in breaking any others. Obviously, SSL is bad news for prospective Internet thieves.

Using simple email forms

Compared to conventional mail, email offers excellent value for money. If you're in business, after completing a sale and obtaining payment, why not email a separate 'Thank you for your order' message to your customer a few days later.

Email offers an effective way of sending messages to other people on the Internet and the Web. Using a secure server, customers can include credit card details and other sensitive information in the knowledge that their security concerns have been addressed properly. This is not to say secured servers are foolproof: no system can offer that; however, breaking through a secure server would take a great deal of computing power, determination and effort.

Installing an email link

The person responsible for entering the HTML code in your Web pages can easily insert the MAILTO command as simple text, or as an icon, or as some other appropriate graphic. After the Web pages are published to the Web, when a customer clicks on the Email link, their browser should display a mail window already set up with address details entered. The customer can then easily type in their message and click the Send button when ready.

If you want to, you can even use the Internet to send a fax. To find out more, point your Web browser at: http:// www.jfax.co.uk

Impress with an Infobot

To those unfamiliar with the phrase, no, an infobot is not some kind of Internet 'Robocop', but rather an automated email-type fax back system. What this means is that when people send an email to you, or to an address you specify, you can arrange for your infobot to reply to them automatically and immediately. This of course, is good business procedure and if you or your staff are otherwise occupied, can help reduce the pressure. Also, of course, first impressions count: we all like to receive prompt replies whether it be email, letter, phone, fax or face-to-face communications.

Make email work for you. Failing to reply to an email is like setting up an 0800 number and then ignoring the phone when it rings.

Infobots can also be set up for other purposes, like automatically uploading a press release to a Web page on a specific date and removing it after a specific date.

To find out more about setting up an infobot, try carrying out a search on the Internet using several search engines to gather information using a variety of techniques.

Traditional contact information

Even though a Web page is an ideal medium in which to carry out transactions using email or through a dedicated Web form, often, customers may still prefer to order by telephone or through the mail. Therefore, it's essential to provide clear and correct traditional contact information on a Web page. However, you could fine-tune contact details to tie in with specific tasks, such as:

- Telephone and fax numbers which deal with accepting payments, with another number for dealing with queries

- Full mailing address for acceptance and processing of payments

- Relevant contact name(s)/department(s)

Although businesses can address the open 24 hours issue using answering machines and automated voice systems, it's well known, customers can become irritated with automated replies, possibly leading to lost sales.

Although it's essential to include contact details at least on the Home page and on any Sales Order pages, many Web page providers include the essential contact details on all Web pages that make up their site. In this way, a Web page provider can be assured potential customers will always have immediate access to order goods or services, or to simply obtain more information.

Addressing the 'open all hours' issue

Including contact information in your Web pages is one essential aspect, but this has implications. Remember, the Internet and Web are 'open' twenty-four hours a day, 365 days a year. Therefore, arguably once you've included this information on your Web pages, the obvious customer service option is to provide backup to match the Internet 'open' times.

In reality, for many individuals, companies and organisations, this is not a practical option. Businesses in particular need to address this issue and decide how to deal with the fact that their presence is available to anyone across the globe with Internet access twenty-four hours a day, every day.

Designing a Web page order form

Doing business over the Internet in the purest sense is not that different from trading using the traditional routes. Using a Web site, you can:

- Display products and services attractively

- Take orders effectively and process them promptly

- Dispatch or deliver the product or service

- Cause interaction and feedback from a customer to take place. *This last item is essential on the Web to maintain a bond with existing clients and build future business*

In this section though, we're concentrating on the second item in the list above. A Web page order form usually comes into play as soon as a visitor clicks on a 'How to Order product' button, or something equivalent. Consider the guidelines below:

1 Clearly define the process through which visitors can choose your products or the services you provide

2 Translate each stage of this process to components in an order form. If you're dealing in products, consider attaching an 'Order this' button (or equivalent) next to each product displayed in your range.

REMEMBER

A secure server is a powerful PC which encrypts sensitive data to deter the criminal element.

3 Draft out first designs on paper. Try out several alternative designs. Consider the design hints and tips given in this chapter and other similar design sources

4 Ideally, test out your designs with a few carefully selected testers to ensure your form meets the needs of your visitors and that you've not omitted anything essential

5 Convert the final designs to HTML and integrate with scripting components. Discuss these aspects with your Internet Service Provider especially during the early stages of your designs to avoid wasting time later

There are several important points to note early on in the design of Web forms:

- Design a form so visitors know what to do every time

- Keep instructions brief

- Make meanings clear in every instance

- Keep the process as simple as possible but adequate for the purpose

Providing a 'Cancel Order' option

Human beings are complex; sometimes we may decide to do something then simply change our minds. Or we may realise we've simply made a mistake in ordering. From a Web form design aspect, we would do well to accept these vagaries simply for what they often are: simple errors. It's a good idea, therefore, to always include a component – such as a Cancel button – whereby a visitor can cancel an order:

- After entering their order details, should they choose to do so

- And even after the order has been sent

- Optionally, you could include a written pledge allowing cancellation without penalty within a reasonable time (also, see the Remember note in the margin).

For businesses selling products, make the process of ordering easy for customers by including a 'Buy this' button after every product description in your Web page catalogue.

When crafting the text content for a 'Cancel order' button, don't forget to relate this to any Sale of Goods laws that may apply in your country, state or area, if necessary.

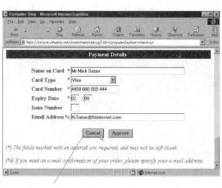

A transaction Cancel button

It's better for you as the vendor (less administration time is wasted) and it's better for your customers. It also shows you've invested time and consideration addressing how to deal with simple mistakes to the benefit of all.

Setting up shop the Wizard way

Any business faced with the task of setting up a Web page-based display of products with access to a secure ordering and transaction facility, normally requires access to people with skills in:

- Database programming

- Installation of a database on a secure server

- Ensuring high security applies in the areas of product viewing, ordering and transacting

Virtual Internet Limited is one company providing these services. However, their 'Wizard' approach can make the job much easier. Here's how it works:

 Using Wizard-based software, such as that available from Virtual Internet Limited, setting up a Web shop is much easier. After you've completed the sequence, your online store can be up and running quickly.

 To see a demonstration or to find out more information about the Virtual Internet Wizard approach, point your browser at: http://www.vi.net

After your account is set up, you can enter company details and Web page colours

2 Then add your product categories

3 Next, add each product for the chosen category, including details and descriptions

4 Now view and check the results from the start

5 Choose a category of products

 The online merchant product referred to on this page from Virtual Internet Limited, also allows you to monitor order and payment details and to regularly download the online ledger covering your transactions.

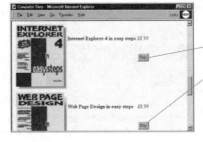

6 Click here to purchase items

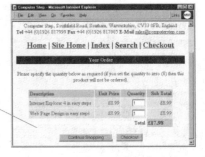

7 Check your order details, then click to go to the checkout

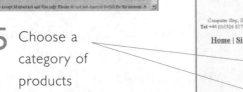

8 Enter address and payment details and click to send order

9 Await order confirmation (just seconds away)

10 Check your online ledger and optionally download data

Getting paid

If you're selling a product or service, getting paid is crucial whatever methods you use to deliver your wares. If you're involved in a business which is not totally Internet-based, then you probably already have several payment options already established. But what if you want to set up a system to accept payments through your Web pages. There are several ways of getting paid over the Internet, although probably the best and quickest is for your customers to submit their credit card details. However, for purchases of less than about £5, it's questionable whether this method is cost effective.

Banks are also conscious of the sensitivity of setting up credit-card-type payment facilities and consequently, for smaller businesses, this type of facility may not be easy to arrange. So what's the answer? The following section attempts to provide one possible please-all solution.

 Another payment option which may be appropriate for some businesses, is to set up a deposit account for a customer. Then, when the customer orders from a Web site, the amount is transferred from their deposit account to pay for the goods.

HANDY TIP

Providing payment choices: some current options

One approach is to design your page to prompt visitors to enter specific details of their order and their contact information including telephone and email addresses if available. Then provide your customer with several payment choices, such as the three options below:

- Option 1: a customer enters their credit card details (on your secure server, of course). After your customer hits the 'Send' button at the bottom of the form, their order is encrypted and sent immediately, providing the fastest payment route

- Option 2: here the customer can omit credit card details, but include specific contact telephone and fax numbers. Explain that once a customer hits this 'Send' button, a representative will contact them shortly to take down credit card details over the phone

- Option 3: provide a facility whereby the order information and credit card details can be printed out and sent either by fax or mailed to the desired payment address

HANDY TIP

One benefit of hosting a Web store for some businesses, is that they may not even need to be concerned with inventory. When a customer orders, the Web store administrators contact their supplier who can send the goods direct to the customer.

HANDY TIP

If you're interested in the Wave Systems microbilling system, view the Wave Systems Web site by pointing your browser at: http:// www.wavesys.com to learn more.

A universal payment system: coming soon perhaps

One system currently being hyped is the concept of microbilling using cybercash. Here, goods and services of *all* prices can be paid for without having to resort to the use of physical money or credit card details – at least not on every transaction. Here's how it could work. One such system is being developed by Wave Systems in the USA (see margin for Web site address). The Wave Systems microbilling method comprises of two main elements:

- The WaveMeter IC – this deals with transactions, credit balance monitoring and data encryption, and is installed at the computer or workstation end

- WaveNet – a central resource which administers the entire WaveMeter network

The key point is this method could be set up to handle both small and expensive purchases. For small purchases, the required amount could be debited from the credit amount stored in the WaveMeter chip. Periodically, the WaveMeter chip could be recharged with new credit probably through the Internet. For the more expensive purchases, the microbilling system could work in combination with conventional credit-card-type transaction systems.

Payment through mediators

Another idea already being used in the USA is to use a mediator which takes credit card payments from the customer, who is then given a virtualPIN number. As the seller, you then obtain the virtualPIN number from the customer and send this to the mediator for payment. The mediator responds by sending an email to the customer to confirm payment. If the customer responds, the mediator handles all the financial side of the transaction for both parties. The goods can then be dispatched.

Whatever system is eventually adopted, much of the transaction processing will become automated to such an extent that it becomes almost invisible, indeed, for most purposes, irrelevant. Fast, reliable and secure transactions is really all that matters to all parties involved.

Promoting your Web pages

With your page design complete and your Web pages published to the Web, first, congratulations! But there's still much you can do to let other people know about what you're offering. In this chapter, we introduce ways to promote your Web site and examine the powerful search engines and what they have to offer. Finally, we take a look at ways in which you can find out what people really think about your Web site.

Covers

Six essential steps | 182

Introducing the search engines | 183

Registering your Web presence | 185

Monitoring Web page visits | 186

Chapter Seventeen

Six essential steps

To gain most from your Web pages, you need to actively promote them. There are several ways in which you can do this; your choices depend on whether your Web pages are business oriented or more for personal or hobby use. Either way, you could try the following procedure:

1. Seek out complimentary Web sites from which to link to your Web pages. Once you've discussed this with the Webmaster at those sites, you can include a link to their Home page

2. Create an electronic business card: a brief text message, 4/5 lines describing your Web site and other essential contact information. Add this to the end of all emails you send

3. 'Register' or broadcast your Web page with multiple search engines correctly. This topic is examined on page 185

4. If you're promoting a business or other organisation, often you can gain greater exposure for your Web site through more traditional routes. Write a press release about your new Web page(s) and send this to carefully selected sources

5. Newsgroups and mailing lists can provide another avenue of promotion - if used with consideration. Newsgroups and mailing lists are simply the Internet equivalent of clubs. People who share a common interest or have something to say can post articles; start and take part in discussions; seek help to solve a problem and announce something new. However, don't even think of advertising in the conventional sense; unwritten rules exist here and these need special consideration (see the beware icon in the margin of this page)

6. Many people like quizzes, contests and promotions. By hosting and regularly updating something appropriate like this, you can gain greater interaction with your visitors to stimulate and maintain further interest in your Web pages

Introducing the Search engines

A search engine is a continually updated directory made up of hundreds of thousands, sometimes millions of Web pages. One of the best ways for anyone to find specific information is to use the search engines. However, you can also record your Web pages. All you have to do is to enter your details on the registration pages and the providers then do the rest. Registering a Web page is covered in depth on page 185.

HANDY TIP **When thinking of words and phrases for your search, it's a good idea to note down several perhaps complimentary words and phrases that could point to what you want. For example, if you want to search for *global warming*, you could also try *ozone depletion*.**

HANDY TIP **Don't forget the Internet Yellow Pages – the Internet equivalent of the Yellow Pages telephone book. Yell is one such popular UK Web directory available at: http://www.yell .co.uk/**

Using the search engines

Search engines although very powerful in scope, are easy to use: simply enter the words or phrases that represent what you want to seek, next click the 'Search' button then sit back and watch the magic work! However, the power of a search engine needs to be carefully focused to get the best return on your time invested. Remember, the Internet can be likened to a vast unordered library in which new books appear continuously, other books disappear and others may seem to 'move' around without warning. This is why search engines are amongst the most effective tools.

The trick is to think of precise words that you want to look for, *not* descriptions or concepts relating to what you want. Also, think of alternatives. For example, for those in the UK, if you wanted to search for 'Football', remember, this represents American football in the USA, so try entering 'Soccer' as well. Often, you can also specify how to filter out data that you're not interested in. Therefore, before going online, it's a good idea to spend a little time thinking about and noting down various keywords and phrases that you intend to use.

Deciding which search engines to use

Most people who regularly use search engines tend to develop one or two favourites. Popular search engines include those in the following list with their Web addresses (or URLs) shown in brackets:

Before searching, if you're unfamiliar with the search engine you've chosen, spend some time reading the accompanying Help text explaining how to use the search engine. By knowing how to fine-tune your searches, you can get better, quicker results, saving you both time and money.

- Alta Vista (http://www.altavista.digital.com)
- EuroFerret (http://www.muscat.co.uk/euroferret)
- Excite UK (http://www.excite.co.uk)
- GOD (http://www.god.co.uk)
- HotBot (http://www.hotbot.com)
- InfoSeek (http://www.infoseek.com)
- Lycos (http://www.lycos.com)
- Lycos UK (http://www-uk.lycos.com)
- Magellan (http://www.mckinley.com)
- UK Plus (http://www.ukplus.co.uk)
- UK Search (http://www.uksearch.com)
- WebCrawler (http://webcrawler.com)
- Yahoo UK (http://www.yahoo.co.uk)
- Yell (http://www.yell.co.uk)

Once your Web pages are published to the Web, make sure they're kept up to date; protect your initial investment. Also, it's a good idea to change Web pages regularly to stimulate new interest.

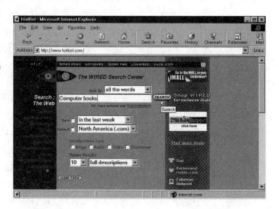

HotBot: provides access to over 54 million documents

Registering your Web presence

So now you're at the stage of completing your Web page design and have uploaded or published your pages to the Web: congratulations! One of the quickest and easiest ways of letting others know about your Web page is to register it with as many search engines as possible. For maximum impact, register your Web page on each and every search engine that you know of. To do this, carry out the following steps for each search engine you want to register with:

 If you don't want to spend time registering your Web page with multiple search engines, companies exist online who will do it for you. For example, you could try: http://www. submit-it.com

 To advertise your Web pages as much as possible, use every available conventional means. Businesses can include Web addresses on all business stationery, in newsletters, brochures and in press releases, at trade shows and exhibitions, and so on.

The Yahoo UK registration page

Find your category, then click here to add your page

1 In your Web browser, locate and enter the URL for the search engine you want

2 With desired search engine opening page displayed, choose the option referring to 'registering a new Web site'

3 Enter your Web site details. Usually, you can enter the name of your Web site or page, your Web and email addresses and other basic contact details, and then you can often categorise your Web page using keywords as well as enter a few sentences describing your products or services

4 When complete, choose the 'Submit' button or its equivalent to register your Web presence

Monitoring Web page visits

If you host your Web pages with an Internet Service Provider, it's worth checking what extra services they can provide. Some can not only log the number of 'hits' to your site, but also provide demographic data such as where your visitors are located, and so on. For businesses, this represents hot information!

A Web page counter does exactly what its title suggests: it allows you to count the number of visits to your Web page or site and display the results. The position of your counter is determined by the HTML code so you can place it as you would any other graphic element.

In a multi-page Web site, it's also possible to have several counters on different pages, but each would need a different reference in your HTML code. The counter design can be simple, or ornate and complex. By varying the design in relation to the rest of your Web page, you can make a counter stand out, or make it take a minor role by blending it in with the page content.

Installing a Web page counter

If you want to include a Web page counter, you need to talk to your Internet Service Provider. Some will install a counter for you and can provide various reports on Web page accesses. Although you can include the HTML code for your counter, because a counter integrates with your Internet Service Provider's Web servers, they may also need to carry out some set up work. Liaise closely with them.

Thank you for buying this book. I hope the information, hints tips and techniques provided, can help you to produce successful Web pages. If you have any comments, good, bad, or otherwise, please let me know. You can contact me through the publishers by emailing: publisher@ computerstep.com

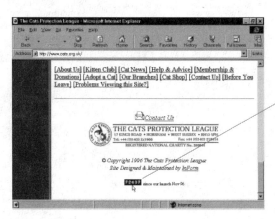

Using unique reply references

If you're providing some interactive element in your Web site, like quizzes or prizes, here's another way to test your Web page response. You can invite people to reply to your address, stating a unique reference number along with the other information you're requesting. You'll know respondents could only have seen this reference on your Web site. In this way, you can build a profile of who your contacts are, where they live, their interests, and so on.

Index

.MID file format   103, 106
.WAV file format   103, 106
3D Web pages   21, 120

A

ActiveX components   94, 134
Adobe Acrobat format   50
Advertising
    Writing the text content   159
Advertising caution
    Newsgroups and mailing lists   15
Advertising corporate presence   23
Analysing visitors' online expenditure   156
Animation
    Benefits   21, 94
    Selecting what to animate   95
    Usage caution   31, 96
Animation techniques (dangers)   87
Assessing business strengths   152
Assessing competitors   154
Audio components
    Basics   102
    Providing background sounds   106
    Usage hints & tips   105
    Usage options   102
    Voice   104
Audio streaming (live)
    Benefits & drawbacks   103
    Browser requirements   107
Audioconferencing   111
Avatar, defined   111
AVI file format   115
Avoiding dead URLs   124, 135

B

Brainstorming for design ideas   44
Branding   45, 155
Browsers   18, 19, 34

Business transactions   43
Businesses on the Web   42
Button toolbar   75
Buttons   125

C

Cacheing images   140
CGI   129
CGI script, defined   165
Check box (Web page form)   166
Checking and testing   45
Client pull technology   135
Colour as a signpost   140
Colour depth   40, 58
Colour perceptions   48
Colours, working with   48
Commercial Web sites
    Assessing benefits against risks   28
    Defining objectives   29
    Profiling visitors   145
    The importance of planning   42
Company mission statement   132
Competitions. See Contests
Competitors' Web sites
    Learning from   32, 154
Compressing files   54
Computer virus risks   168
Contact details   132, 174
Contacts page   148
Contests   147
Copyright issues   24, 63, 110, 132
Corporate Web site design   43

D

Data encryption   172
Design pointers   32
    Learning from the artists   46
    Using active space   46

Design strategy, establishing   32
Designing for readers' needs   37
Digital watermarks   64
Domain names   26
Dynamic GIFs   86, 87

E

Effective Web page design   22
Electronic brochures   36
Electronic business cards   137, 182
Email   173
   Access   21
   Addresses   26
   Benefits   136
   Dedicated email software   137
   Electronic signature example   137
   How it works   136
   Installing a Web page email
     link   136, 173
   Providing a marketing link   143
   Providing an electronic
     signature   137, 182
   Simplifying business transactions   157
   Using to win orders   173
Example Internet business   44

F

FAQ lists   146, 162
Flashing components
   Benefits   88
   Some implications of using   88
   Usage caution   31
Flowcharting in page design   32
Font styles   141
Fonts   49
Forms
   Components   166
   Design hints & tips   169
   How they work   165
   Including a link to a form   132
   Including tables in a form   76
   Introduction   164

   Nesting one inside another   169
   Sending data content using
     email   164, 168
   Usage benefits   164
   Web forms server   165
Frames
   Applying to a Web page   83
   Avoiding too many   84
   Borderless   81
   Custom border   81
   Different types available   81
   Download time implications   81
   Floating   81
   Introduction   80
   Linking   81
   Multiple   80, 81
   Popular uses   80
   Usage benefits   21, 83
   Usage drawbacks   83
   Usage implications in non-compatible
     browsers   82
   Using with a background image   70
Frequently Asked Questions. *See* FAQ lists

G

GIF image format   54, 55
Good design objectives   33

H

Hidden field (Web page form)   166
Home page (commercial)
   Benefits and drawbacks   128
   Caution   129
   Including traditional press coverage
     content   128
Home page (personal)
   Deciding content   126
   Including personal photographs   127
Home page design
   Deciding content   124
   Including a link to a form   132
   Including a toolbar   125

Keeping clutter free   45
Planning   124
Prompting visitors to bookmark   127
Providing an index   132
Stating browser support   124, 125
Home page design (commercial)
Assessing skills required   129
Home page link   148
Horizontal lines   50, 72
Hosting a Web page: the options   25
HTML   12, 13, 17, 19
<A HREF=...> command   115
<APPLET> tag   92
<BGSOUND> tag   106
<BODY BACKGROUND= ..>
command   70
<D> tag (Definition List)   78
<EMBED> tag   90, 98
<MARQUEE> tag   35
<NOFRAMES> tag   84
<OBJECT> tag   94
<OL> tag (Ordered List)   78
<PRE> tag   77
<SCRIPT> tag   93
<TABLE> tag   74
<UL> tag (Unordered List)   78
Affects of different browsers   13
ALT attribute   56, 57
Definition list commands   78
Introducing   19
Levels of headings   50
LOWSRC attribute   60, 61
V4.0   39
Hyperlink   19
Hypertext link. See Hyperlink
HyperText Markup Language. See HTML

I

Image size, considerations   57
Imagemaps   62
Images
As language barrier breakers   54, 55
Caution with photographs   62, 63

Colour and bit depth relationship   58
Format conversion, advice   58
Interlacing benefits   60
Making transparent   61
Pixel measurements   59
Using cartoons   62, 144
Using line art   62, 144
Using previews   63
Wrapping text around   51
Images types   54
Improving customer services   23
Infobot systems   146, 173
Information content   36, 145
Interactive
components   133, 134, 146, 182
Interlacing   60
Internet access   14, 15
Internet basics   8, 10
Internet commerce
Current popular businesses   23
Internet etiquette. See Netiquette
ISDN telephone line   16, 116, 117

J

Java applet
Caution when using   90, 91
Compatible browsers   91
Described   92, 93
Including in a Web page   91, 92, 134
JavaScript components   84, 93, 134
JPEG image format   54, 56
JScript, defined   93

K

Kb, defined   56, 57
Kilobyte. See Kb, defined

L

Legal pages   43
Links to other Web sites
Caution   24

Lists   21, 77, 78
Log-in pages   43
Logging email addresses   32
Logical design hierarchy
  Creating   36
Logos   38, 55

M

Macromedia Director file format   115
Mailing lists   15, 161
MAILTO command   20, 21, 136, 173
Market research sources   23
Marketing costs
  Reducing with a Web page   152
Marketing with a Web page
  The two-step design plan   153
Modems   16
Monitoring Web page access   186
MPEG file format   106, 115
Multimedia, defined   154, 155
Multiple Web page authors   38
Music components   109

N

Navigation buttons / links   141
Netiquette   15, 182
Netscape Navigator
  Identifying a secure server   172, 173
New design techniques
  Fading   156, 157
  Pop-up windows   156, 157
  Sliding a component into view   156, 157
  Zooming   156, 157
News service components   110
Newsgroups   160, 161

O

Off-screen planning   45
One-browser-only design pitfall   46
Others' Web page mistakes   33

P

Page background, black
  Overlaying with coloured text   68
Page design templates   141
Page length   149
Panoramic video   121
Paper advertisements
  Converting for the Web   36
PDF file format   50
Permits (Web)   24
Pixel, defined   81
Plug-in, defined   90
Plug-ins   94, 95, 96, 97
PNG image file format   54, 56
Poor design characteristics   33
Pop-up menu (Web page form)   166
Press release advertising   182
Preview images   63
Professional indemnity insurance   153
Profiling visitors   35
Promoting Web pages   182
Push technology   14
Push-button, image (Web page form)   166
Push-button, plain (Web page form)   166

Q

QuickTime video format (from Apple)   115

R

Radio broadcasting over the Web   108, 109
Radio button (Web page form)   166
RealAudio file format   106, 107, 108
RealVideo content   116, 117
RealVideo file format   115
RealVideo Player (browser)   116
Registration form   136
Related Web sites   150
Return visits, promoting   133
RGB colour model   59

S

Scrolling menu (Web page form) 166
Scrolling text across the screen 35
Search engines
   Deciding which ones to use 184
   Introduction 183
   Using to find new links 150, 182, 183
   Using to register a Web page 182, 185
Search pages, local Web site 43
Secure server 172, 173
Shockwave components 88, 89, 90
Sound components 21, 102
Sound support requirements 102, 103
Spamming 15
Special Web pages 43
Standing out (design) 154
Supplementary content pages 140
SWOT test, applying 44

T

Table
   Specifying background settings 74
   Specifying border settings 74
Table (HTML), defined 72
Table cell background 74
Tables
   Benefits of using 21, 73
   Changing their appearance 74, 75
   Creating non-uniform Web pages 74
   Design options 72, 74
   HTML- compared to word processor-
     type 72
   Spanning several cells into one 74
   Specifying size in pixels 74, 75
   Widening cell margins 72, 73
Testimonials 132
Testing checklist 45
Text
   Changing its colour 48, 51
   Converting to a graphic 49, 51
   Improving legibility 49, 68
   Summarising its content 51
   Using shorter paragraphs 51

Text entry box (Web page form) 166
Text-only Web sites 48, 49, 52
Thumbnail images. *See* Preview images
Transacting business on the Web 130
Transparent images 61
Twenty-four hour businesses 174

U

Unusual file formats 97, 98
User registration pages 43

V

Video components
   Benefits & drawbacks 114
   Including in a Web page 115
   Usage hints and tips 118
Video formats 115
Video resolution 40
Virtual Reality Modelling Language. *See*
   VRML
Virtual shopping: an example 177
VRML 121, 122
   Commercial applications 122
VRML Plug-ins 122

W

Web page
   Helping visitors focus on content 88
Web page background 66
   Converting to black 68
   Creating from an image 70
   Creating watermark-type graphics 70
   Maximising contrast 66
   Overlaying images 69
   Using an embossed image 67
Web page contests 147
Web page counters 186
Web page CVs 41
Web page design
   Building around a theme 41
   Buying in skills 13
   Considering content balance 36

Establishing appropriate content 142
For marketing purposes 152
keeping business payments simple 36
Linking to the familiar 158
Providing a focus 36
Providing consistency 38, 140
Providing extra value 156
Ten key words to aid success 159
The value of open space 31
Using humour 144, 154, 155
Using professionals 36
Visitor oriented design techniques 37
Web page design software 17, 18, 19
Web page design: individuals 41
Web page development 134
Web page image & status 44
Web page newsletters 75
Web page order forms 175, 176, 177
Web page payments 179, 180
Web page security 43
Web pages
Benefits 10
Benefits (commercial) 11
Considering corporate policy 24
Customer-friendly design 30
Defined 12
Environmental benefits 10
Establishing purpose 36
For text-only viewing 31
Introducing 12–13
Legal issues 24
Providing frameless versions 80
Providing the right information 30
Providing your own Internet
connection 17
Publishing to the Web 17
Reasons for creating 28
Requirements for creation 16
Testing with several browsers 18, 19
Three rules to aid success 28
Typical components 21
Updating designs 31
Web purchasing: motivators 159
Web server, defined 18

Web site (business)
Benefits 11, 42
Estimating running costs 43
Web site (general)
Options for setting up 13, 142
Web site cooperatives 150
Web transactions 42, 43
Web video technology 114
WWW 12
Finding images libraries 60
Locating marketing information 152
RealAudio Web site 107
Sony's Web site (RealAudio
samples) 108
What's new on the Internet 130